PANICS & CRASHES
and How You Can Make Money Out of Them

Other Books by Harry D. Schultz

Panics & Crashes and How You Can Make Money Out of Them

Harry D. Schultz

Arlington House   New Rochelle, New York

Second Printing, June 1972

Copyright © 1972 by Arlington House, New Rochelle, New York.

Library of Congress Catalog Card Number 76-186242

ISBN 0-87000-147-7

MANUFACTURED IN THE UNITED STATES OF AMERICA

Contents

flation, 1914–1965. . .Inflation, 1940–1968. . .The Schultz Gold Portfolio. . .Facilities Swiss Banks Can Offer You

Of all the peoples of history the American people can least afford to condemn speculation in those broad sweeping strokes so beloved of the professional reformer. The discovery of America was made possible by a loan based on the collateral of Queen Isabella's crown jewels.
N. Y. Stock Exchange Economist

1
Introduction

Uneven economic and political development is an absolute law of Capitalism.
Nikolai Lenin

EVER SINCE the markets in stocks and shares began, panics and crashes have been a periodic phenomenon. Lenin, in the days of the Russian revolution, noted this, implying that the business cycle was a crime to be eliminated in the perfect world of future communism. It therefore seems strange (and a trifle disconcerting) that today's politicians of the capitalist societies have come forward with aims and claims for ironing out the business cycle which are identical to those of Lenin some 50 years ago.

CAPITALISM AND THE BUSINESS CYCLE

Suddenly in a world where even Russia is adopting certain aspects of capitalism, our Western politicians have condemned the business cycle as a criminal offense and one they "will no longer allow to occur."

In this book we shall examine past panics and depressions of history to see what caused them, and whether they *are,* as Lenin claims, an integral part of capitalism. If this is true, and if you try to iron them out, perhaps you remove capitalism itself, and replace it with some form of socialist society.

By definition panics and crashes are the results of human nature, weaknesses, and/or mistakes, rather than "acts of God." A business cycle in olden days tended to be the result of periodic famine caused by weather, population factors, and even more human problems such as war and riot. But industrial panics and crashes are completely man's doing. They are his answer to a given set of

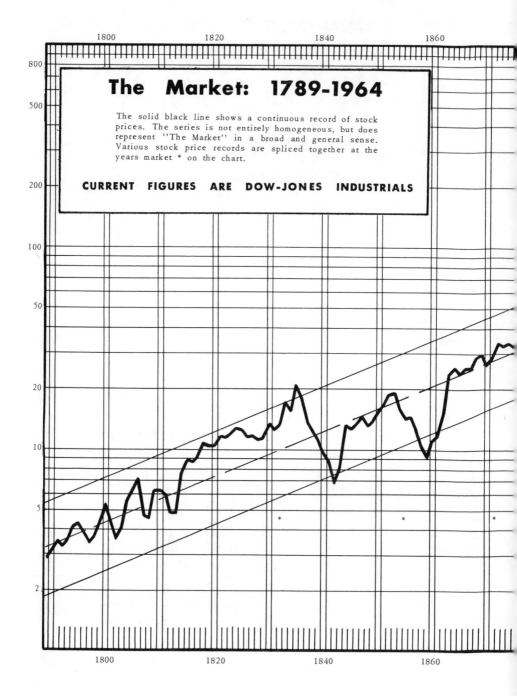

The Market: 1789-1964

The solid black line shows a continuous record of stock prices. The series is not entirely homogeneous, but does represent "The Market" in a broad and general sense. Various stock price records are spliced together at the years market * on the chart.

CURRENT FIGURES ARE DOW-JONES INDUSTRIALS

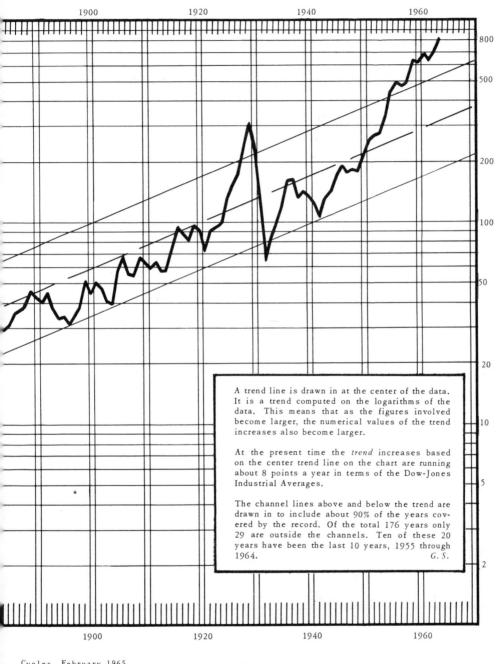

A trend line is drawn in at the center of the data. It is a trend computed on the logarithms of the data. This means that as the figures involved become larger, the numerical values of the trend increases also become larger.

At the present time the *trend* increases based on the center trend line on the chart are running about 8 points a year in terms of the Dow-Jones Industrial Averages.

The channel lines above and below the trend are drawn in to include about 90% of the years covered by the record. Of the total 176 years only 29 are outside the channels. Ten of these 20 years have been the last 10 years, 1955 through 1964.   *G. S.*

circumstances when he behaves in an emotional rather than a rational manner.

In the sense that only UNDER capitalism is man *allowed* personally to make his own mistakes, and has the *right* to panic if he wants to, and to "put his money where his mouth is," then Lenin was completely right.

MARX AND CAPITALISM

Marx predicted that capitalism would ultimately destroy itself, that business cycles would get longer and be more explosive, until there would arrive a sort of Armageddon when the final crash would dissolve the world into "glorious revolution." There are those among us who look at the nineteenth century with its small, sharp, and very frequent panics and crashes and relatively small wars, and compare it with the twentieth century with its two major wars and one major crash — and shudder as we realize that perhaps Marx could be right.

Is he? Or is it that the misguided politicians of today who believe that they *can* iron out the business cycle for all time are denying the nature of the beast, and that all they are doing is prolonging prosperity at the expense of future chaos?

In other words, could it be that "the permanent plateau of prosperity" concept is basically a *socialist* concept of unreality? And in trying to achieve it, do they build the prosperity on an increasingly unsound basis, so that when the end comes they may find that they have played completely into communist hands? One cannot set up a new form of government without first destroying the old one; the best way to do this is to destroy the *economic* foundations of the country. I quote Lenin again: "Political institutions are a superstructure resting on an *economic* foundation."

THE USES OF PANICS

We shall examine panics, crashes, and the business cycles of this century and the last, to see if there is any similarity between them, to see if perhaps they all happen for the same reason or, at any rate, for rather similar reasons. Like the child who puts its hand on a hot stove and thereby learns never to do it again, perhaps panics occur to define for man the *limits* (in business) to which he can go and survive. Perhaps government intervention stops this from happening and thus denies man the right to set these limits for himself. Maybe they serve as a safety valve. Or perhaps it is that government has nothing to do with it. Perhaps we should have *more* government. Maybe government could, as is fashionable today to claim, iron out the business cycle for all time? Perhaps man is really so nearly perfect that he does not need his limits to be drawn for him. Perhaps along with the "barbaric metal," lack of discipline in man is a thing of the past? We'll see, as pages speed by.

We shall see just how people in the past did survive and even prosper in the various panics. In every human holocaust some survive. Somehow they have the ability to "swim upstream," to keep a cool head when those around them panic. They do this by examining not only the facts of the situation, but by studying the psychology of those who are *instinctively* doing the wrong thing.

Hence in order to survive, and indeed make money in a panic and/or crash, one has to examine very thoroughly, not only the occasions in the business and civilization cycle which make for a panic, but to what extent people are likely to "overkill" at such times. When man panics, he doesn't just panic to the extent of trying to save himself, but somehow he allows the emotion to run wild, and so becomes subconsiously bent on self-destruction.

PANIC A PRIMITIVE EMOTION

Because of our primitive heritage, we have the ability to panic built into us as a safety measure, not as a device for our destruction. Emotion produces in the body powers it does not have at normal times. Adrenelin is one such power. For example primitive man faced with a tiger could run much faster than he could at normal times. This was how he survived, and if there was no place to run, then the extra power gave him additional fighting ability. The problem is that in modern civilization panics do not call for physical exertion in most cases, and because he uses *less* physical energy, man seems incapable of determining when the need to panic is *over*. It is as if primitive man, when he ran away from that tiger, used his extra energy to run until he dropped dead from overexertion.

It didn't happen then, but it does happen today. For man, when he takes flight in a metaphorical sense, just doesn't stop running. So we end up with a panic being much bigger than the reason for the panic would warrant.

Hence we reach the first rule for beating a

panic. Never underestimate its size. Don't calculate what a "reasonable reaction" is. Calculate rather to what extent man is prepared to destroy himself before his reaction to the situation has run its course.

The second rule, which particularly applies today, is: Never underestimate the power of the politician. One *can* say when a balloon has gone past the safety level in size, but it is difficult to predict when it will burst. This is the way the politicians' modern attempt at "permanent prosperity" seems to be working.

In times of panic one has to cease to be an investor and become a psychologist. Values of shares, price/earnings ratios, stocks looking cheap, etc., mean very little or nothing. The only thing that matters is the *panic-factor* in human nature.

THE PANIC-FACTOR

We shall try to examine the panics of the last 150 years to try to measure this panic-factor in man and see if we may discover some yardstick with which we can measure how certain types of depression, recession, and monetary crisis will produce certain degrees or types of panic. Also we shall try to measure (when politicians forestall the inevitable) how much they are *able* to postpone cause-and-effect reaction and how much they will ultimately have to cope with when the delayed disaster appears.

When talking about panics today it is amazing to learn that people seem to have heard only of 1929. It is as if there has never been another panic in the history of U.S. or world markets. As you read further you will see just how untrue that assumption is. In the 200 years of the U.S. stock market there has been a panic of major magnitude at least *every 20 years,* and minor panics as close together as about every 5 to 10 years.

This means that unless you were too stupid to be frightened when they happened, or unless you understood panics and sold at the right time, then the whole concept of making money in the market is a myth. Indeed most brokerage house figures will show this, that 95 percent of the people do not sustain gains in the market. The reason is obvious: the *panic-factor* about which so little is said or understood. Yet in order to make money consistently the panic-factor should be studied to enable us to panic less when others panic more.

I

PANICS
LISTED

2

The Age
of Corruption

*Banking Establishments are
more dangerous than standing armies.*
Thomas Jefferson — Letter to
Gerry

THE NINETEENTH CENTURY in America was splattered with the blood (literally and figuratively) of men who went broke during any of its various speculative orgies. This was a century of very dramatic panics which in many cases were directly the result of government crossing swords with big financiers. Of course the stock market was very much smaller than it is today, so every stock behaved a bit like our present day over-the-counter stocks. The corners, the bear raids, and other sorts of manipulation made the fluctuations much wilder than they would have been otherwise. However, contrary to general belief, this was not an era of total laissez-faire; far from it. In the strict sense government has *never* left America alone, right from the beginning of its financial history, but rather, has intermittently tried to "help" things along, invariably with disastrous consequences.

GOVERNMENT INTERVENTION IN THE NINETEENTH CENTURY

It is fashionable today to look back on the nineteenth century, when big bankers were encouraging speculation, as an age when corrupt men unbalanced the economy and caused devastation. However, I hope to prove in the next few chapters that this is just not true, in the strict sense. Obviously, most had self-interest at heart, and easy money schemes have always seemed a way to solve financial problems. However, one has to look at the nineteenth century as an era without a Federal Reserve Bank, and without the SEC. These two bodies have not reformed anything; they simply took away from the big financiers their job of controlling stock purchase and money supply, and took on the job themselves. Government then proceeded to "solve" problems in exactly the same way as the big financiers did. Easy money and Keynesian theories are not new. What is new about them, in the U.S.A., is that the power to expand money was considered better placed in the hands of government — but that expansion was always practiced from the beginning of American history. (Furthermore, corners and bear raids were not eliminated by government regulation; they just take a more sophisticated form now.)

But let us examine a few of the panics of the nineteenth century to see exactly what happened. You'll see frequent similarities with today and you'll observe that human nature makes them occur, regardless of laws and circumstances.

PANIC OF 1837

During the 1830s Nicholas Biddle rose to be the greatest banker in America. He ruled the money world with the hand of an aristocrat. He dazzled the men of his time with his abilities and personality and he became president of the Second Bank of the United States. President Jackson feared the bank, because money is power and that much financial power in hands other than government was obviously unnerving to the government. Jackson decided to wage war on the bank. His official excuse was that the bank had failed to establish a sound currency, for throughout the 1830s speculation was rampant. But his real desire was to close the bank at any price and under any pretext. He vetoed the renewal of the bank's charter. Biddle, not to be easily outdone, divorced the bank from the sponsorship of federal government and obtained a charter for his bank from the Commonwealth of Pennsylvania. With no federal restraining hand on the bank, Biddle was now able to expand the bank's activities considerably. He embarked on speculation and encouraged admirers to do the same. He was particularly interested in land speculation, and a major land boom began soon afterward.

Land became a mere vehicle of speculation, not an investment. In other words, people bought land with the sole idea of selling it at higher prices. This of course meant that the buyers did not care whether they were getting value for money, merely that they could sell again to somebody. Hunger for land led to hunger for money. Specie (gold and silver backing) was fairly plentiful in seaboard cities, but west of the Alleghenies it was often still in the form of Spanish milled dollars and other foreign coins. Therefore money was manufactured daily in the form of currency notes. *Demand* seemed to be the only control on the amount of money issued. There were 634 banks in the country, with loans of $525 million. But the specie backing these loans was only $38 million, a position which continued to weaken.

The battle between Biddle and Jackson continued apace and this animosity split the banking groups of Wall Street into two camps.

In 1836 Jackson publicly condemned the rush for public lands and issued a specie circular demanding that payments for land should be made only in specie or notes with 100 percent specie back-

ing. He prohibited the deposit of federal revenues in
Biddle's United States Bank and distributed government revenues among state banks who were on his
side.

This obviously served as a wet blanket to
dampen the ardor of speculation in land and shook
confidence in the circulating notes. The situation
was further complicated by the bankruptcies of several important mercantile houses in England toward
the end of 1836, which cut down the demand for
American cotton and thus depressed the U.S. cotton
industry.

However the panic itself arrived with brutal
suddenness on Friday, March 17, 1837. The combination of extended credit and cutbacks in demand for
cotton caused the biggest cotton houses in New Or-
leans to go under with staggering losses. Nearly one-
fifth of the bank directors were insolvent. The city's
commerce was in awful shape. Its indebtedness in
liabilities of cotton factors and land speculation was
stupendous, approximating $200,000,000. New Or-
leans banks stopped payments in consequence of the
failures of the cotton houses. This in turn caused a
fall on Wall Street to depths that had never been seen
before. There was a fearful crisis on the money market.

Bank failures mounted. Silver and silver
change disappeared from circulation. This caused
widespread alarm. Financial chaos engulfed the entire country. The influx of capital from Europe
ceased. The entire South went bankrupt. Nine tenths
of the merchants in Mobile, Alabama suspended operations. Men with real estate enough to pay their
debts 20 times over were failing, because *specie* currency was the order of the day, and credit could not
be created even on real estate. The bankers sus-

pended specie payments. Riots were feared and troops were called out. In 1841 the United States Bank revealed that out of precrash assets of $74 million it could only exhibit $12 million in active capital. It went under.

PANIC OF 1857

The California gold rush occurred immediately prior to the panic of 1857. The discovery of gold on the West Coast encouraged people to move West in ever-increasing numbers and of course this led to vast speculation on the railroads, to build transport to and from the newly opened regions.

Wall Street had never known such prosperous days. Business boomed and, as usual, people's enthusiasm ran away with them, and credit became overextended. Bankers were ready to loan on almost any description of paper. It is said that brokers with only $1,500 on deposit drew checks for $100,000 and even $300,000 which were promptly certified by paying tellers. Mining schemes, railway enterprises, sugar, cotton, and lead operations sent men on speculative binges which in normal times no man in his right mind would consider. As things became more hectic, extra shares (mainly in railroad stock) were floated, with little or nothing to back them.

The worst of these was the New Haven Railroad where $2,000,000 of stock had been forged. A grave crisis in credit and confidence occurred. Many brokers were suspended. The stock market collapsed and banks called loans. There were panics in Cincinnati and other cities.

Within 10 years California had produced gold

dust and nuggets to the value of $555 million. But all this wealth had become a commodity for export. Trusted heads of corporations in effect had swindled investors in their own securities. Throughout the business world, both large and small shared the same desire to get rich quickly. Clerks had stolen while their superiors swindled.

The failure of the Ohio Life Insurance and Trust Company in August 1857 was the last straw which actually precipitated the panic. Its liabilities were $5 million. There were runs on other banks. Mills closed because there was no money to pay employees. The paper inflation of the country was estimated at $2 billion, a much larger sum than all the gold currency derived from Australia and California combined. Bank after bank suspended specie payments until finally the Bank of New York, the strongest and oldest in the city, failed.

The crisis ended at last, and the city resigned itself to accepting bank notes as a circulation medium. The Chemical Bank alone continued to pay out gold.

The whole debacle was caused by human nature reacting to the gold discoveries and railroad building — which in turn stimulated speculation and inflation far beyond what was realistic. It led to frauds and deep social corruption to the point where the people imagined that prosperity would last forever, expanding rapidly and used in ways previously known to be totally unsound.

DEPRESSION OF 1861

The first economic effect of the Civil War was to throw the North and West into severe panic. At the outbreak the agricultural South owed northern merchants close to $300,000,000, practically all of which was a total loss to the North. At the beginning of the war, uncertainty about the future brought about a wave of retrenchment and economy. The banks were caught with cash reserves far too small to meet such an emergency. All of these factors united in bringing on the depression of 1861.

In 1861 there were nearly 6,000 failures of northern firms in the amount of $5,000 or more. Northern banks were able to maintain specie payment until the latter part of December 1861 when they were forced to suspend payment, which was followed almost at once by like action of the federal government. In the South, except in New Orleans, suspension occurred immediately after the opening of the war and continued until the end. The wildcat banks of the West were especially hard hit, not only because of their methods of banking, but also because of their intimate relations with the South. In Illinois 89 out of 110 banks failed, while 39 in Wisconsin and 27 in Indiana went under. However the depression of 1861 quickly gave way to a wartime revival of prosperity. The South however was not so fortunate. There the war meant destruction, chaos, a currency that finally had no value at all, and a long, long grind before a revival was possible. During the four years of the Civil War, government expenditure in the North was greater than during the whole previous history of the nation.

One of the primary methods the government chose to raise money was by issuing, for the first time, non-interest-bearing notes (greenbacks) and this created an inflationary condition that took decades to overcome.

PANIC OF 1873

The Panic of 1873 was brought on chiefly by
unrestrained speculation in railroad construction
and wildcat investment in business schemes in a variety of ventures. It cut across the thirteen years following the Civil War, separating an era of luxury and
prosperity from one of hardship and poverty.

When the struggle ended at Appomattox, the
economic strength of the North had, not surprisingly,
also suffered and there was a recession which was
apparent in 1865 and which built up into the great
trade depression of 1868.

From 1869 to 1873, however, business showed
abounding prosperity and to many the crash of Jay
Cooke's banking house was, when it came in 1873,
like a bolt from the blue.

The main cause was the failure of the federal
government to check inflation during boom years. In
1868, an act was passed in Congress, by a large
majority, suspending any further contraction of the
currency, and leaving a huge volume of wartime
greenbacks reduced by only about one fifth. The
value of greenbacks in terms of gold had risen
markedly from the wartime low but the currency
was far from stabilized. Everywhere there was currency inflation, with rising prices. Railroads were
being overbuilt (the mileage was doubled), importation of luxuries from Europe was excessive. Federal
and state spending had become outrageous. David A.
Wells, Special Commissioner of the Revenue, said in
1869 that men were idly drifting from pursuits directly productive of goods to occupations connected
with commerce, trade, or speculation.

In 1868 federal notes in circulation equaled

$356 million and by 1872 Secretary Boutwell had increased this total most considerably. This bloated the credit system and, together with the uncertainties of the situation, encouraged speculation. Population in the major commercial centers increased and the number and cost of business buildings rose markedly. In 1870 there were 431,000 business firms in the United States. By 1871 there were 609,904. This was more than just healthy growth. It was an unhealthy madness for trading and gaming, induced by an inflated paper currency. Moreover, the violent ebb and flow of this inflated currency in the financial capital of the world at that time, New York, was responsible for wide oscillations in the money market and consequent disturbances of a grave nature.

Since notes of the national banks were legal tender in payment of all debts, they tended to accumulate each winter and summer in New York, while in the late spring and autumn, especially autumn when crops where being moved, money became scarce. Thus at one period speculation flourished and the price of stocks and bonds rose to excessive heights; then the ensuing stringency compelled all holders to sell, with the result that prices fell unduly low. The wheat and corn buyers of the West and the corn factions in the South could hardly find any currency to pay for the crops and they had to sell the crops again at once because their banks were unable to get adequate credit in New York, receiving delayed payments and lower prices than world markets justified. The farmers could not meet their debts with the storekeepers, nor the storekeepers with the jobbers. In all, the monetary and credit system was radically defective and this was certain to accentuate any passing crisis. Fear gripped the business community when it was realized that any break in the inflated structure might cause a crash if all creditors demanded cash payment at once.

To add to the dangers of the situation there was, in addition to the foreign money flowing into the country to finance the railroad construction and other schemes, a considerable imbalance of imports over exports. As a result, gold was being drained out of the country to make up the unfavorable balance of trade and to pay the public and private debts which had been incurred. The great quantities borrowed abroad in 1861–1868 had left the U.S. with obligations reaching $1.5 billion. This meant an annual interest charge in 1868 of $80 million and other payments, quite apart from those made for ordinary imports, brought the total annual levy to about $130 million. Big sums for those days.

For a time after the war, foreign demands were met by a transfer of government bonds to European account, but this resource soon came to an end. It thus became necessary to export specie, and this disturbed the U.S. money market. The grave financial situation became more perilous as the 1870s moved on. By February 1873, the best commercial organs were expressing their apprehension of the crisis. Inflation and credit had by this time reached an unprecedented high. Total credit was six times greater than total cash and widespread bankruptcies were inevitably to follow. In the five years from 1868 to September 12, 1873, the national bank deposits increased only $43 million, but bank loans for the same period rose by $283 million. In other words, the aggregate *debt* had risen 50 percent while the aggregate circulating *capital* had increased only 7½ percent. Since all of the debts of the country had to be paid out of the circulating capital, the danger was clear.

Meanwhile, the number of failures and crises increased each month. In 1871 there were 2,915 failures. In 1872 there were 4,069, involving a loss of more than $121 million. On the railroad front, the burden of paper was growing constantly heavier; the wildcat methods and frequent exposures undermined the confidence of foreign investors and the companies were forced to obtain their credit at home. In 1872, of 364 listed railroads, only 104 paid any dividends at all and 69 percent of these paid less than 10 percent. More and more straws were piled on to the camel's back. The fires in Portland, Boston, and Chicago almost touched off the final crash. Only the intervention of the government, Jay Cooke (grown powerful since his successful marketing of war bonds for the federal treasury), and other strong financial interests saved the situation. In the spring of 1873, money markets were so badly shaken that associates of Jay Cooke begged him not to carry forward the Northern Pacific syndicate, then being formed.

Throughout the first half of 1873 the Credit Mobilier scandal was gathering force, throwing Congress into a state of demoralization and accentuating the general distrust of big business. Meanwhile, New York had been agitated by news of banking scandals, causing further severe strain on the money market, already inadequate to sustain the top-heavy structure of debt. The crash had to come but no one expected it to be as devastating or as long lasting as it was.

Matters came to a head in September 1873. On September 8 the New York Warehouse and Security Company failed. Five days later Kenyon Cox and Company failed. Rumors spread that other major companies were in serious danger. On Wednesday,

September 17, the bottom fell out of the New York
stock market as prices tumbled; stocks came down
with a clatter. In all the offices which had burdened
themselves with unmarketable collateral, consterna-
tion reigned. Reports of the panic spread to Boston,
Washington, and Philadelphia where President
Grant had just arrived to spend the night at Jay
Cooke's home at "Ogontz." The banking house of Jay
Cooke was generally considered unshakable.

Just before eleven o'clock next morning,
Thursday, September 18, the doors of his New York
office were suddenly closed. This step, taken by the
partner in charge after consulting with a group of
bank presidents, electrified the city. It was an admis-
sion that they were unable to obtain cash for their
loans and investments and, therefore, could not pay
back to depositors their savings on demand. Jay
Cooke, in tears, had to order his Philadelphia office
closed. A few minutes after noon, the Washington
branch of the First National Bank shut, making the
suspension complete.

The New York Stock Exchange was in an
uproar "such as the oldest member could never
remember hearing"; stocks and bonds crashed, selling at any price to anyone who had cash to buy. In
Philadelphia, the telegraph bulletin from New York
caused the entire stock board to rush pell-mell into
the street and down to Jay Cooke's doors to verify the
report. A newsboy shouting "all about the failure of
Jay Cooke" was arrested by a disbelieving policeman.
In Washington, news of the failure reached a criminal court during a murder trial and it was hastily
adjourned. Judges, lawyers, and spectators hurried
into the avenue to learn further news.

Bank after bank barricaded doors against the
angry crowds of depositors whose savings were

wiped out. Bankers, desperate to get cash to cover the paper in their vaults, demanded payment on loans to manufacturers and on mortgages to farmers. Unable to pay, the farmers lost homes and acreage. Businessmen lost their factories for which no payment with cash could be found and their employees were thrown out of work to join the farmers in destitution.

The real fright and dismay of the failures lay in the fact that the aggregate indebtedness of the business world was far too great to be paid out of the circulating capital. Once this was known, every businessman clutched at his means of payment. There was a frenzied rush for ready money; the weaker were trodden ruthlessly underfoot and the panic was under way. There was nothing to be done but to let the storm blow itself out. Several houses failed the same day as Jay Cooke's and there was a steady succession of crashes. Fiske and Hatch went down in New York, carrying with them all hopes of an immediate financial reorganization of the prostrate Chesapeake and Ohio. The Lake Shore Railroad failed; the Union and the Nation Trust companies were forced to suspend.

At 11:00 A.M. on the third day of the panic, September 20, the governing committee closed the New York Stock Exchange, an unprecedented step, taken "to save the entire street from utter ruin." On the fourth day, President Grant, Secretary Richardson, and other high government officers met Commodore Vanderbilt and other financial leaders at the Fifth Avenue Hotel. As a result, the stock exchange was closed for ten days; the banks pooled their resources and issued, for the first time, clearinghouse certificates; the government released 13 million greenbacks from the Treasury for the purchase of government bonds. All of which had little effect. They were

short-term measures for a short-term crisis. The
economy was desperately sick and, like all patients
on the danger list, needed careful nursing and a long
convalescence in order to return slowly to health.

The year ended with more than 5,000 commercial failures, with liabilities totaling more than
$228,500,000, or nearly twice as much as the previous
year. There were 89 railroads defaulting on their
bonds, including the Boston, Hartford & Erie, the
Kansas Pacific, the Northern Pacific, the Missouri,
Kansas & Texas, and the Rock Island. The total bond
issues on which interest payments were suspended
amounted to very nearly $400 million. Deposits in the
northern banks had fallen off more than $100 million
during the second half of 1873. More and more firms
failed and the depression grew. There was vast
unemployment and railroad building stopped. In
1874, only 1,940 miles of road were built — one third
of the average of the preceding five years. All industries connected with railroads, rolling mills, machine shops, foundries, followed suit and either
ground to a halt or cut their production drastically.
Subsidiary industries shut down one by one as demands and payments for the goods failed.

In 1874 there were 5,800 failures; in 1875, 7,700;
in 1876, 9,000; in 1877, another 9,000. Most railroads
went into bankruptcy. Unemployment far out-
stripped the ability of charities to relieve hunger and
destitution. Breadlines formed everywhere. Poverty
abounded, and there were many demands for relief.
Between 1873 and 1878 imports dropped to a record
low. For example, importation of silk dropped by one
third; that of tea dropped by half; no carpets at all
were imported. Wages were low, work was virtually
impossible to obtain. Commodity prices dropped,
rents fell, and luxuries had no market. Furniture and

clothing became cheaper. In the first calendar year following the panic, Americans retrenched their private expenditure by not less than $400 million. Gradually, sanity revived and stability returned, but it was a long, slow haul and many wealthy railroad magnates stood in breadlines before the corner was turned.

Although, superficially, the cause of this depression appeared to be overspeculation, like other panics, it was basically caused by inflation in the form of excess currency printing and overextension of credit. However, as always, this overextension had been based on a certain amount of genuine prosperity. But man endlessly goes too far in the name of greed. The Civil War had created an unreal prosperity. Feverish industrial and agricultural activity had taken place in the North during the Civil War, and was aided by rising prices due to inflation, created to pay for the war.

When the war was over immense regions of the West had been opened to agriculture, and the easy profits of war prosperity had been invested freely, mainly in the railroads. The superficial prosperity had been too rapid, the speculative expenditure too extensive to be healthy. Enormous amounts of capital had been sunk in railroads to finance the 30,000 miles of track built between 1867 and 1873, and little immediate return could be expected from this trackage. The opening of lands had thrown older areas out of cultivation and decreased their value. Speculation had become rampant and the morality of politicians and capitalists decreased as the prosperity mounted — hardly a new phenomenon. But as with all eras of credit-made booms, there is a limit. The money becomes a narcotic which is needed in ever-increasing amounts to keep up the expansion;

and then one day things collapse. The panic of 1873 was no exception.

PANIC OF 1884

While we seem to be establishing that all panics are basically monetarily induced, the panic of 1884 was more classically of this type than most. That is, it was almost entirely a financial disturbance rather than an industrial one. Its effects did not slop over into business in quite the same way that panics before and later did.

It arose primarily out of the vast money manipulations of the "young Napoleon of finance," Ferdinand Ward, who built a house of cards on the foundations of General Grant's confidence and credulity. The crash of Grant and Ward brought down banks and brokerage houses, and as usual a whole series of high level thefts and peculiar speculations were uncovered, but the crash did not seriously affect industrial conditions.

Hetty Green, a sinister female Wall Street speculator, did her bit to help the debacle along by suddenly calling for $25,000,000 in securities and $475,000 in cash from the prominent firm of J. J. Cisco & Co. which forced the bankers to close their doors. The shock to the security markets was severe, but its effect was over comparatively quickly.

The savior of the situation was J. Pierpont Morgan, who had come into financial prominence at about this time. However, failures occurred at intervals throughout the summer of 1884, culminating in the closing of the Wall Street Bank due to the irregularities of its cashier.

PANIC OF 1893

The panic of 1893 was precipitated to some degree by the results of the presidential election of 1892, which heralded a modification of the government's tariff policy. Also there was the apprehension that the gold standard could not be maintained. Grover Cleveland was elected that year on a Democratic platform committed to a reduction of the tariff, a prospect which manufacturers contemplated with dark forebodings. Cleveland himself believed in the gold standard, but his party was shot through with inflationary fiat money sentiments. To complicate the difficulties, the federal cash surplus of the 1880s had been wiped out by the extravagances of the Harrison administration and by the McKinley tariff of 1890. An act of 1892 authorized the Secretary of the Treasury to suspend the issue of gold certificates whenever the amount of gold coin or bullion in the Treasury reserved for the redemption of U. S. notes fell below $100,000,000. Added to this problem was the Sherman Silver Act of 1890 which compelled purchase of heavy amounts of silver to be paid for by Treasury notes, redeemable in gold. Of course this siphoned gold out of the country.

As we can see, yet another panic was shaping up, based solely on the manipulation of money. As usual the climate of easy money set the stage for overspeculation among the investing public. In the early months of 1893 money had been drained from Wall Street for the supposed working of tin mines in South Dakota, and for the buying of Florida lands. The latter venture caused new towns to spring to life all over Florida. Then the trouble started. In early 1893 the Philadelphia and Reading Railroad and the

National Cordage company failed. It seemed to be
the signal for a downturn. Other opportunists' projects began to falter. Plants closed; monopolies exploded one by one. The shrinkage of money values
had immediate repercussion upon the banks, and a
large number closed their doors in New York, followed by banks all over the country. Again inflation
was getting out of hand. Depositors crowded the
counting rooms of savings banks. Drained and
frightened banks exercised their lawful privilege of
withholding payment. Merchants and manufacturers by the thousands were forced to the wall. Every
company failure swelled the ranks of the unemployed. Hungry workmen rioted in the streets of New
York and Chicago. Ready money became shockingly
scarce. Gold was still sweeping out of the country.
Government statements asserted that there was $17,-
000,000 more money of all kinds circulating in the
country than the month before, but frightened folk
began to hoard their dollars. Money in small denomi-
nations was bought and sold at a premium in Wall
Street.

Alarmed by the flight of gold, the U.S. Senators
repealed the Sherman Silver Act. During 1893 over
600 banking institutions failed, and during the summer 74 railroad corporations, owning 30,000 miles of
track, passed into the hands of receivers. By June
1894 at least 194 roads, operating 40,118 miles, had
failed. More than 15,000 commercial failures were
recorded for 1893.

President Cleveland was determined to maintain a gold standard, even when gold stocks fell below the danger level. Various tactics were tried to
bring the gold reserves up, but bullion continued to
drain away.

In 1896 an unexpected upturn in wheat prices

led to the election of McKinley, and business and the stock market picked up smartly. Two years later, successful termination of the Spanish–American War stimulated the industrial activity of the country, and industry rose to levels unheard of in previous times. The United States was hailed thoughout the world as a leading power and a land of incomparable prosperity.

3
The Age of American Greatness

The Business of America is Business.   Calvin Coolidge

THE FINANCIAL history of the twentieth century can really be divided into two parts: the first part being the age when capitalism, hand in hand with industrialism, went forward to make America a power in the world; and the second being after 1929, when government felt it necessary to interfere in a big way and to attempt to do for people what they had managed quite successfully to do for themselves up to that point. The first one-third of the century certainly had its bad spots but, as before, they were caused more by government intervention than by the so-called brutality of capitalism and the business cycle.

In this chapter we shall discuss the main panics from the beginning of the century until the granddaddy of them all, 1929. Many show conditions which are akin to those of today. Nothing *really* changes.

PANIC OF 1901

The 1901 stock market panic came without warning. So say the books on the subject. What this means of course is that the *majority* of people, as always, did not read the signs, and *they* lost money. In this sense *all* panics come without warning — it's the element of surprise that makes people act first (that is, panic) and think afterwards (if indeed they think at all). Prior to this break, one of the wildest bull markets in the history of Wall Street had taken place, and the peak of the pyramid was the cornering of the Northern Pacific Railroad. Contrary to general belief, corners are not merely the way in which idle speculators fleece the general public. Rather they are, or were (now the SEC won't allow them!) the way that *control* of a company was fought for, and the 1901 corner was of this type.

The fight for control was between the Morgan–Hill interests and the Schiff–Harriman contingent. An artificial corner in this stock forced the price in a single day from $170 to $1,000, principally due to short covering. As Northern Pacific climbed, the rest of the market fell through the floor, with leading shares dropping 50 to 75 points during that hectic session. Call money went from 3 percent to 70 percent.

The biggest problem was that a great number of people had sold Northern Pacific short. Therefore as the stock climbed, both brokers and broker's customers could do virtually only one thing: sell other shares they owned in order to cover. The next day the contending groups patched up their differences and allowed the remaining shorts to cover at $150 a share. Many large-scale operators were ruined as a result of the Northern Pacific battle, and countless margin traders were wiped out. But the damage done to the banking and industrial structures of the country was very slight. Except for a comparatively brief setback in 1903, the country experienced an almost uninterrupted interval of six years of prosperity.

PANIC OF 1907

The year of 1907 opened with strained and mysterious movements in the money markets. The problems were put down mainly to President Theodore Roosevelt's antagonism to business which caused him to meddle and restrict where otherwise business would have gone its own way, resolving through evolving. However, like all other panics, there was a triggering "straw that broke the back," and in this case it was the affair of Amalgamated Copper Company. This company controlled a majority (50 to 60 percent) of U.S. copper production. In theory, to maintain the price of copper at a more remunerative level in the face of a weak market, Amalgamated Copper kept copper off the market during the months of April–September 1907 by stockpiling it. In this way they kept the price of copper artificially high. In the meantime a group of three men — Morse, Heinze, and Thomas — were gaining control of eight New York banks.

In September the stockpiled copper was unloaded, and naturally the price of copper and copper shares broke. Heinze, who was then interested in copper and apparently not knowing of the stockpile, tried a sales plan to bull the market with the result that he and his brother's brokerage firm went broke. To try to bull the market Heinze used funds obtained from Morse, and Morse in turn had illegally obtained these funds from the banks he controlled. The depositors in the Morse banks became alarmed at the situation and the banks were forced to apply to the clearinghouse for aid. This was granted (on the expulsion of Morse, Heinze, and Thomas) and by October 20 the minor disturbance was thought to be over.

However, the president of Knickerbocker Trust Co., third largest bank in New York, with deposits of over $62 million, was also supposed to have certain business connections with Morse. On October 21 the National Bank of Commerce refused to clear for Knickerbocker, which caused a run on Knickerbocker. By now a panic was on and demands were for cash.

The Panic of 1907 has been called the "rich man's panic," because it did not involve the entire country as most others have done. However, the fact that such a panic was possible showed up flaws in the banking and financial system, which directly led later to that action of dubious benefit, the Federal Reserve Act.

But what was wrong with the system? How could a small banking war cause a major panic? What had government done or not done? A strong cyclical economic expansion began in 1905. The money market came under fairly severe pressure in the autumn of 1905 but nevertheless the boom continued until early 1906. By this time credit was tight and pressing hard against the level of required reserves in New York, and the stock market was weakening. Early in 1906 bank reserves in New York revealed a deficit. It was at this point that Secretary of the Treasury Shaw decided to take action. He set out to support the money market by transferring funds from within the independent Treasury to national banks where they were held as public deposits, and by encouraging the purchase of gold from abroad. The problem was that the drain of gold from Europe to the U.S. provoked retaliatory action in Europe. Both England and Germany sharply raised their discount rates. At this point gold started to be exported. Hence in effect Shaw prolonged the boom into 1907 when all normal signs pointed to business topping out a year earlier. The consequence was a more disastrous collapse in 1907. Again government tampering not only failed but created a climate for abuse and made economic and financial matters worse.

After the Panic of 1907 Congress appointed a

National Monetary Commission to study the whole question of improvements in the banking system. So conscientiously did the commission perform this task that nearly 50 volumes were produced on its findings. However, never did it occur to anybody that the fault could lie with the too-easy ways of *creating* money and credit, both of which the public seemed to clamor for. In this atmosphere the Federal Reserve Act was born in 1913. We shall discuss this act in a later chapter.

PANIC OF 1913

Disturbing rumors of the possibility of war began to develop in 1913. Although officially discounted and not taken completely seriously by the American public, business became apprehensive and conditions in the United States began to weaken, and then went from bad to worse. Commodity prices broke. Unemployment and company failures spread. The stock market crashed. When war was declared in August 1914, business was paralyzed, and the stock market went into complete chaos. The New York Stock Exchange, and the other exchanges as well, closed from August to November.

However, the crisis was relatively short-lived in terms of stock prices, and conditions in the United States showed a sharp comeback as war orders poured into the country from Europe, revitalizing industry and finance. The government's inflationary policy for financing the war added to the impetus at this stage. Government Liberty Bond campaigns educated the public at large into the intricacies of invest-

ing and speculating, a fact which was ultimately to
reap a grim whirlwind in the late twenties.

PANIC OF 1921

The end of World War I stalled the machine of
production, and manufacturers and retailers were
caught with high inventories which could not be
moved. Commodity prices started to move downward. But export business eventually picked up and
a postwar boom started. However, the basis of this
boom was thoroughly unsound. It was based on U.S.
government loans to the Allies who then used them
to buy American goods. But European finance was in
chaos, currencies were in disorder, and devaluations
occurred. Unfortunately, the U.S. answer to the situation was to lend more money, which meant that
America imported the instability of Europe, and did
not devalue to counteract it. By 1920 money in circulation in the United States and bank credit were
enormously expanded as compared with prewar conditions. Prices were high because of overexpansion
of money.

By 1920 the export balance of the United States
was completely abnormal based on the strange situation that she was selling her goods abroad with her
own money! This meant that America lost not only
goods but gold too, and the loss of goods further
raised prices and brought about inflation which encouraged speculation. In the two years following the
war the U.S. government spent almost as much
money as it had spent during the war years. As usually happens during periods of inflation it becomes
increasingly difficult to get a dollar's worth of work

for a dollar's pay. This is best illustrated in this period by the fact that despite nearly four million men returning to industry after the war, production actually *declined!* And of course profits started to vanish as industry began to spin its wheels.

The rubber band stretched tighter and tighter. The U.S. government cut back on its loans to the Allies. Europe with exchange rates against them, did not have enough money to make extensive purchases abroad. This cut the market for American manufacturers and brought disaster to many American farmers. By 1920 the postwar boom had attained totally unhealthy proportions. Credit expansion had reached the legal limit and the banks were forced to retreat. Manufacturers became convinced that they had produced more than could be sold. Wholesalers and retailers looked suspiciously at inventories and began to cancel orders. With these factors at work the market broke and the business cycle pursued its downward swing.

PANIC OF 1929

Possibly more has been written about this particular debacle than any other in American financial history; and yet, while more dramatic than those that preceded it, the basic causes were about the same.

There is no one factor to account for the stock market crash coming in October. It was long overdue. However, the general public had been so schooled into believing that they were on a permanent level of prosperity that few believed it marked the beginning of the worst depression the United States has ever experienced. Most of them in fact believed that it was

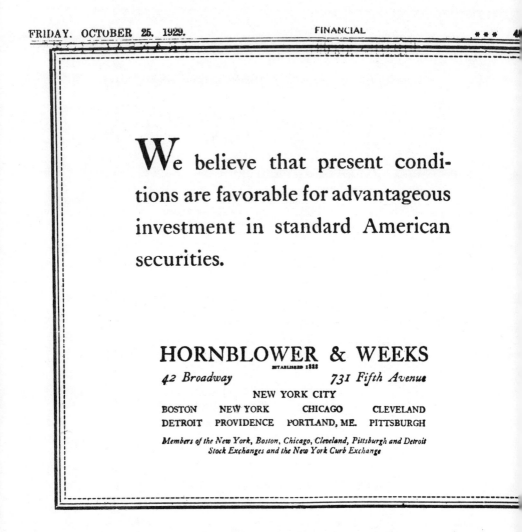

An expert's view. The ad of a major brokerage house on the day after the crash.

merely a temporary setback in a permanent uptrend.

The idea of the "new era," which many believed had definitely arrived, was too strongly embedded in the consciousness of the American public. It seemed impossible that the lofty structure of production and profits reared by the hands and brains of the country could be shaken down.

The prosperity which developed in the 1920s after the 1921 break was primarily in the automobile industry and the accompanying boom in road building. It was also characterized by a boom in urban construction, resulting from the scarcity which developed during the war years. There was widespread demand aided and abetted by installment buying of new products such as radios and household electric equipment.

Favorable trade balances enlarged an already unprecedented abundance of gold and on this basis credit expanded and trade developed. Private loans on a large scale were made to Europe and South America and the proceeds were spent largely in the U.S. Despite real evidences of prosperity sufficiently numerous to give the decade an appearance of a boom era, fundamental flaws existed in the economic structure. Certain industries, notably coal mining, textiles, shipbuilding, railroad equipment, and leather manufacture failed to revive after the postwar depression. More important was the failure of agriculture to respond to postwar economic recovery. Unemployment was high — running well above 1½ million — throughout the 1920s despite the boom. The domestic picture showed chronic depression in certain industries and overexpansion in others.

However, the wealth of the nation and the real income of large numbers of people was increasing, which in its turn caused the increase in speculation.

VOL. LXXIX....No. 26,206.

"All the News That's Fit to Print."

The New York Times.

Copyright, 1929, by The New York Times Company.

NEW YORK, THURSDAY, OCTOBER 24, 1929.

TWO CENTS In Greater | THREE CENTS Elsewhere | FOUR CENTS Elsewhere
New York | Within 200 Miles | Except 7th and 8th Postal Zones

PRICES OF STOCKS CRASH IN HEAVY LIQUIDATION, TOTAL DROP OF BILLIONS

PAPER LOSS $4,000,000,000

2,600,000 Shares Sold in the Final Hour in Record Decline.

MANY ACCOUNTS WIPED OUT

But No Brokerage House Is in Difficulties, as Margins Have Been Kept High.

ORGANIZED BACKING ABSENT

Bankers Confer on Steps to Support Market—Highest Break Is 96 Points.

Frightened by the decline in stock prices during the last month and a half, thousands of stockholders dumped their shares on the market yesterday afternoon in such an avalanche of selling as to bring about one of the widest declines in history. Even the face of seasoned, dividend-paying, shares were sold in reckless fashion. The low was a tremendous smash, and the result was a tremendous smash in which stocks lost from a few points to as much as ninety-six.

Loss in Market Values.

The absolute average decline on the

HOOVER REVEALS PLANS TO DEVELOP INLAND WATERWAYS

In Louisville Speech He Outlines Project for Trunk Systems to Cost Half a Billion.

URGES ST. LAWRENCE WORK

Would Turn "Swords to Plowshares" With Money Saved If London Parley Succeeds.

ENDS OHIO RIVER TRIP

President Starts for Capital After Being Acclaimed at Madison, Ind., and Louisville.

From a Staff Correspondent of The New York Times.

LOUISVILLE, Ky., Oct. 23.—President Hoover tonight stated the policies of his administration in respect to the great national waterways of the country. This was his first speech on the subject since his inauguration and it was made as a part of the celebration here of the completion of the Ohio River.

He discussed the Mississippi waterway system, the St. Lawrence River and the question of "private enterprise in substitution for government operation" of barges and other craft. He suggested a nine-foot depth in the Mississippi trunk system, and said that the United States should undertake to do its part in the removal of obstacles in the St. Lawrence to ocean-going vessels inward to the Great Lakes.

The President outlined a five-year plan under which, including $10,000,000 annually for the St. Lawrence, the government would add $20,000,-

---

College Sports Tainted by Bounties, Carnegie Fund Finds in Wide Study

Survey of 130 Schools Shows One in Seven Athletes Subsidized— N. Y. U., Fordham, Columbia, Harvard and Princeton Are Accused—'Slush Funds' and 'Recruiting' Indicted.

One athlete out of every seven engaged in intercollegiate competition is "subsidized" to a point bordering on professionalism, says a report on "American College Athletics," made public yesterday by the Carnegie Foundation for the Advancement of Teaching after a survey which has consumed more than three and a half years and entailed visits to 130 colleges and secondary schools.

The athlete, the report states, completes for no other consideration than athletic ability whether it be in the form of "athletic scholarships," "slush fund," supplied by loyal alumni and local tradesmen, or in other cases on loans provided through the athletic "host" upon American college sport. The report asserts. Those engaged in "the nation-wide commerce," of recruiting and subsidizing—alumni, athletic director and subsidizing, the very root of the manifold defects of American college athletics.

At Fordham University, the report asserts, forty scholarships are provided from athletic funds to provide for needy athletes who sometimes repay the educational assistance from the cost of tuition, board and room for needy athletes who sometimes repay the educational assistance individual alumni. Well organized systems of recruiting were noted at Columbia University, but that

ties where abuses exist, the report continued.

"Bulletin 23," as the report is called, represents the first comprehensive study of American college athletics and their effect upon the minds, morals and physical well-being of undergraduates. Making its appearance in the midst of the football season, it is certain to become a center of a stormy discussion any student, it frankly discloses any attempt to rate institutions according to prevalence or absence of abuses, freely as examples of specific practices.

For instance, at New York University, it is said, coaches award most of the limited number of scholarship to athletes with the administrative officers of the university maintaining as many low-pressure turbines in such a manner that not only will speed be increased but fuel consumption reduced to. This institution, too, the report asserts, has maintained prominent athletes in squad enrollment until they were ready to enter the university and continue on

Special to The New York Times.

WASHINGTON, Oct. 23.—Herbert C. Lakin of New York, president of the Cuba Company, an American corporation having property on the island estimated to be worth $175,000,000, told the Senate lobby investigating committee today that after recent experiences with tariff legislation he had "sorrowfully" reached the conclusion that an American company whose interests could not be assured of proper protection unless it maintained a lobby in Washington.

Continued on Page Twenty-two.

$1,000,000,000 TRAFFIC PLAN FOR CITY READY FOR MAYOR; TUBE UNDER 5TH AV. URGED

MEETS 20 YEARS' NEEDS

Vast Scheme of Routes for Vehicles Links Five Boroughs.

BATTERY-BROOKLYN TUNNEL

One for Length of Island Under Fifth Avenue Proposed at Cost of $200,000,000.

GREAT DRIVE IN BROOKLYN

Connects Borough and Queens —Program Drafted by Day and Zimmerman After Survey.

Special to The New York Times.

PHILADELPHIA, Oct. 23.—A program for traffic relief in New York City based upon a survey intended to take care of the city's needs for the next twenty years and involving the expenditure of more than $1,000,000,000 would be the materialized in the voluminous report prepared by the engineering firm of Day & Zimmerman, Inc., and ready for submission to Mayor James J. Walker.

The report recommends a comprehensive scheme for the construction of vehicular tunnels, bridges, through and marginal highways and

---

CUBAN SUGAR LOBBY HAS SPENT $75,000 SEEKING TARIFF CUT

H. C. Lakin of Cuba Company Tells Senators 11 American Firms Raised $95,000.

LINKS NATIONAL CITY BANK

Witness Frankly States the Aim Was Lower Duty—Press Office Was Maintained.

GEN. CROWDER JOINED FIGHT

Sliding Campaign Attributed to Hoover — More Testimony Heard on Eyssen's Activities.

NO WORD OF DITTEMAN; HOPE FOR HIM FADES

The Montana Cattleman Who Started Across Atlantic Is Long Overdue.

ODDS AGAINST HIM HUGE

British Seek to Add 2½ Knots To Speed of the Mauretania

Special Cable to The New York Times.

LONDON, Oct. 23.—An attempt to increase the Mauretania's average speed two and a half knots by utilizing waste heat now going up the funnels, it was stated today, will be made the next time the Cunarder is drydocked for overhauling.

A new device to 1½ incorporated in the engine room is successful, it is held that the Mauretania will be able, in its twenty-second year, to resume its former speed decline on even terms.

Engineers have found from the experiments made on the furnaces to the low-pressure turbines in such a manner that not only will speed be increased but fuel consumption reduced by about 5 per cent., or $5,000 on a single trip, is believed. But any attempt will be made to lower the Bremen's record before Spring.

COALITION BREAKS OVER CARBIDE RATE

13 Democrats, 3 Republicans, Desert at Senate Rejects, 42 to 37, Halving of Cent Duty.

POWER ISSUE IN TARIFF

Norris Says Big Companies Back Duty and Reminds Copeland of Smith's Stand.

Thyroid Determines if a Man Should Be a Flier, Says Dr. Asher

Special to The New York Times.

BALTIMORE, Md., Oct. 23.— Upon perfect thyroid condition depends an airplane pilot's efficiency, declared Dr. Leon Asher, Professor of Physiology at the University of Berne, in an address last evening before the Physiological Society of Medical School of Maryland University.

Individuals with a hyper-thyroid or hypo-thyroid secretion have no place in aviation, he continued.

Dr. Asher said he found in experiments that animals with more than the normal thyroid secretion resist the effects of low oxygen, and are not able to withstand an atmosphere of low oxygen content, such as is met in high altitudes.

The same is true of man, he said.

BRITAIN IS WORRIED BY BRIAND'S FALL

Sees Young Plan Agreements and Naval Parley Endangered by Shift to Right.

BANKERS TURN BACK REPARATIONS ISSUE

Organizers at Baden-Baden Decide Hague Parley Must Define Collection Program.

FRENCH LOSE TO GERMANS

BERLIN ALSO FEARS CHANGE

Dr. D. C. Miller Declares Ether Drift Found; Reports Experiments Contradicting Einstein

Whalen Gets Private Fund for Air Police; Will Buy Three Planes and Train Nine Men

Continued on Page Two.

Continued on Page Four.

Continued on Page Twelve.

Continued on Page Thirteen.

Continued on Page Fifteen.

Continued on Page Two.

The New York Times.

"All the News That's Fit to Print."

THE WEATHER

Cloudy and continued cold today; tomorrow fair and warmer.

Temperatures yesterday—Max. 59, min. 47.
NOV. 1 Weather Forecast—1r unin on Page 22.

VOL. LXXIX...No. 26,207. NEW YORK, FRIDAY, OCTOBER 25, 1929. TWO CENTS In Greater | THREE CENTS Elsewhere New York | Within 200 Miles. | Except 7th and 8th Postal Zones

Copyright, 1929, by The New York Times Company.

WORST STOCK CRASH STEMMED BY BANKS;
12,894,650-SHARE DAY SWAMPS MARKET;
LEADERS CONFER, FIND CONDITIONS SOUND

Wall Street Optimistic After Stormy Day;
Clerical Work May Force Holiday Tomorrow

Confidence in the soundness of the stock market structure, notwithstanding the upheaval of the last few days, was voiced last night by bankers and other financial leaders. Sentiment as expressed by the heads of some of the largest banking institutions and by industrial executives as well was distinctly cheerful and the feeling was general that the worst had been seen. Wall Street ended the day in an optimistic frame of mind.

The opinion of brokers was unanimous that the selling had got out of hand and not because of any inherent weakness in the market but because the public had become alarmed over the steady liquidation of the last few weeks. Over their private wires these brokers counseled their customers against further distressing selling at sacrifice prices.

Charles E. Mitchell, chairman of the National City Bank, declared that fundamentally the business situation was unimpaired. "The declines of the last few days," he added, "that this reaction has badly overrun itself."

Lewis L. Pierson, chairman of the board of the Irving Trust Company, issued last night the following statement:

"Severe disturbances in the stock market are nothing new in American experience. The pendulum always swings widely and it would seem as though the long-expected break should bring about an equilibrium.

"The position of the Federal Reserve Bank is unusually strong and the borrowings of member banks are moderate.

"Considering the record-breaking earnings in many industries, we may well remember that when fundamental values are lost sight of by the unthinking majority it is time for courage on the part of those investors who have a real sense of basic worth."

Because the clerical facilities of brokerage houses are overtaxed as a result of the recent phenomenally heavy trading, an agitation was started yesterday in favor of a suspension of trading on the New York Stock Exchange tomorrow.

It is thought possible that the governing committee will take action today, without waiting for a petition from the membership. In many brokerage houses the posting of books has fallen far behind and some relief will have to be afforded, according to brokers, unless the market quiets down shortly.

FINANCIERS EASE TENSION

Five Wall Street Bankers Hold Two Meetings at Morgan Office.

CALL BREAK 'TECHNICAL'

Lamont Lays It to 'Air Holes'
—Says Low Prices Do Not Depict Situation Fairly.

FINDS MARGINS BEING MET

Sees Market 'Susceptible of Betterment'—Mitchell, Potter, Wiggin, Prosser at Talks.

Wall Street gave credit yesterday to its banking leaders for arresting the decline on the New York Stock Exchange, when the stock market was being overwhelmed by selling orders. The conference at which the steps were taken that reversed the market's trend was hurriedly called at the offices of J. P. Morgan & Co.

The five bankers who met at the headquarters of the famous private banking house at noon yesterday and again at 4:30 P. M., following the meeting of the board of Federal Reserve Bank of New York, were:

LOSSES RECOVERED IN PART

Upward Trend Starts With 200,000-Share Order for Steel.

TICKERS LAG FOUR HOURS

Thousands of Accounts Wiped Out, With Traders in Dark as to Events on Exchange.

SALES ON CURB 6,337,415

Prices on Markets in Other Cities Also Slump and Rally —Wheat Values Hard Hit.

The most disastrous decline in the biggest and broadest stock market history staged a spectacular recovery in the final trading hour yesterday. In the very midst of the collapse five of the country's most influential bankers hurried to the office of J. P. Morgan & Co., and after a brief conference gave out word that to them the foundations of the market to be sound.

That the market smash has been caused by technical rather than fundamental considerations, and that many sound stocks are selling too low.

Suddenly the market turned about, on buying orders thrown into the

---

HUMBERT ESCAPES ANTI-FASCIST'S SHOT AT BRUSSELS TOMB

Student Slips as He Tries to Assassinate the Italian Crown Prince.

HEIR CONTINUES PROGRAM

He Places Wreath on Unknown Soldier's Grave and Reviews Guard of Honor.

CROWD MOBS ASSAILANT

Italian Came From Paris to Kill Prince During Celebration of Royal Betrothal.

Special Cable to The New York Times.

BRUSSELS, Oct. 24.—Within a few hours of the official announcement of his engagement to Princess Marie José and only a few feet from the tomb of Belgium's unknown soldier, an attempt was made this morning to assassinate Prince Humbert, heir to the Italian throne.

A young Italian law student, Fernando de Rosas, who had come to Brussels from Paris expressly to kill the Prince, confessed that he fired a revolver at him from a distance of twelve feet. Fortunately the assassin missed just as he fired and the shot went wild.

Prince Humbert, unruffled, as his first act in the country of his fiancée bride, laid a wreath on the tomb of the Unknown Soldier. His engagement to the Princess being official, an elaborate ceremony had been arranged. There was a big crowd in the square around the Colonne de Congrès and two companies of infantry were lined up with their flags and the fine of the Italian em-

---

TESTIFIES HE HANDED $10,000 TO WARDER

Dell' Osso Asserts Former State Banking Head Counted Alleged Bribe in Home.

SENT BY FERRARI, HE SAYS

Memorandum on Withdrawal of Cash From City Trust Is Held From Jury Temporarily.

Special to The New York Times.

Gennaro Dell' Osso testified yesterday that he helped to pay $10,000 "in large bills" to Frank H. Warder when the latter was State Superintendent of Banks.

GRUNDY SAYS LOBBY IS NEEDED TO UPHOLD PARTY TARIFF VOWS

Pennsylvanian at Senate Inquiry Asserts Hoover Platform Demands the Rates in Bill.

TELLS OF CAMPAIGN FUNDS

Veteran Lobbyist Active in Raising $600,000 in 1924 and $1,000,000 Last Year.

HITS AT SENATE COALITION

Borah Assailed as Having Reversed Himself From Stand Taken in Campaign.

Special to The New York Times.

WASHINGTON, Oct. 24.—Joseph R. Grundy, head of the Pennsylvania Manufacturers' Association and a conspicuous figure for years in the Republican organization of that State, told the Senate Lobby Investigating Committee today that the rates in the tariff bill were but little more than adequate in accordance with pledges made in the Kansas City platform upon which Herbert Hoover made his successful run for the Presidency. The witness declared that protective duties and that only protective principle, and that if the consumers had wanted lower tariff duties they should have shown it by electing Alfred E. Smith to the Presidency.

Mr. Grundy took sharp issue with "tariff jobbies" since 1887, and frankly said so, insisting that only those interests could be "protected" that they needed at the hands of Congress.

JURY IN FALL TRIAL LOCKED UP FOR NIGHT

No Word Comes After 11½ Hours' Deliberations of 8 Men, 4 Women in Bribe Case.

DEFENDANT STAYS ABED

Exceptions Were Taken by the Ex-Secretary's Counsel to the Judge's Charge.

Special to The New York Times.

WASHINGTON, Oct. 24.—The jury trying the case of Albert B. Fall, former Secretary of the Interior, who is charged with accepting a bribe of $100,000 from Edward L. Doheny, had not reached a verdict late last night at 11 o'clock tonight. It had deliberated since 11:30 o'clock in the morning

---

Plane Lost in Channel Gale;
5 Aboard Fail to Reach Paris

Special Cable to The New York Times.

LONDON, Oct. 24.—The English Channel was being swept by searchlights tonight in a hunt for three British airmen with two passengers who left Croydon airdrome in a new three-engined airplane this afternoon for Paris.

A sixty-mile-an-hour gale was raging over the Channel when the airplane crossed the cliffs near Dover and disappeared into a mist.

The airplane, intended for passenger service in Kenya Colony, was piloted by Captain Campbell Black, and carried G. D. Fletcher, an East African journalist, and R. Rowthorne as passenger. Owing to low visibility at the Croydon airdrome the returning one to Croydon and the third passenger who preferred to travel on the surface.

Load-Speaker Can Be Nuisance, McAdoo Advises Magistrates

The opinion that a radio loud-speaker, under certain conditions, may be classed as a nuisance was expressed by Chief Magistrate William McAdoo in a letter sent to the borough magistrates at the five borough magistrates. His letter declared:

"As you know, there is a widespread complaint all over the city by people who are annoyed and kept from sleeping by the loud-speaking radio in apartments, tenement houses and other buildings. Many complaints come to this office urging me to ask you gentlemen to treat these cases seriously.

"The person who starts a loudspeaker under conditions where it is found to annoy and disturb other people and keep them from proper rest, in my opinion, is guilty of maintaining a nuisance and where the act is persistent and annoys a considerable number of people, he or she can be charged under Section 1,530 with maintaining a nuisance."

Business Weakness.

STILL PLAN TAX REDUCTION

Reserve Board Meets Twice in Day and Keeps in Constant Touch With Markets Here.

STOCKS TUMBLE IN CHICAGO

Selling Swamps Exchange in 1,200,000-Share Day—Part of Big Losses Recovered.

Meeting Essex Tenements.

Missing Lake Ferry Sank With Crew of 57; Four Bodies Found; All Hands Believed Lost

Continued on Page Two.

Continued on Page Sixteen.

Continued on Page Three.

Continued on Page Twenty-five.

Millions of workers and middle-class people who had
never seen a bond or a share of stock until the days
of the Liberty Bonds and the campaigns for employee
stock ownership were now conscious of the stock
market. Following the lead of the professional stock
market speculators, more and more people entered
the market. The sight of these new people in the market was seemingly too much of a temptation for the
many captains of industry.

Soule says "The traditional theory is that business corporations issue stocks and bonds only when
they need additional capital. . . . During this period,
however, new securities were manufactured almost
like cakes of soap, for little better reason than that
there was gain to be made out of their manufacture
and sale." Between January 1925 and October 1929
the number of shares of stock listed in New York
more than *doubled.* The easy money to be made in
speculation as stock prices mounted, stimulated increased interest until speculators talked little about
actual values and thought only about the future
prices they might get when selling the stock. This
could only have one end. It came in October 1929.
However, as always, most people neither saw it coming, nor would they even admit it was happening
when it did happen. A browse through the newspapers of the 1929–1933 era will show how, all the way
down, respected analysts maintained that what was
occurring was a slight adjustment in a permanent
uptrend.

When stocks finally hit bottom in 1933, more
than 83 percent of all value had been lost. Wages
were half what they had been at the top. It has been
argued that had wages been ALLOWED to drop
faster the debacle would never have gone so far, that
the laws of supply/demand would have returned the

situation to normal in a very short time. But that's a maybe.

The crash which wiped out the entire postwar boom caused a depression that lasted for a decade, and also brought in a very different *concept* of American government. The age of American socialism had begun.

The New York Times.

"All the News That's Fit to Print."

VOL. LXXIX....No. 26,208.

NEW YORK, SATURDAY, OCTOBER 26, 1929.

Copyright, 1929, by The New York Times Company.

TWO CENTS In Greater | THREE CENTS | FOUR CENTS Elsewhere
New York. | Within 200 Miles. | Except Tth and 8th Postal Zones

THE WEATHER

Partly cloudy and warmer today;
tomorrow fair.

Temperature yesterday—Max. 54; min. 41.
U. S. Weather Forecast—For details see Page 25.

FALL FOUND GUILTY IN OIL BRIBE CASE; JURY ASKS MERCY

Ex-Secretary, Stunned by the Verdict, Keeps Calm, but Wife and Daughters Sob.

FRIEND FAINTS IN COURT

Defendant, Freed on $5,000 Bail, Is Wheeled From Room and Taken to a Hotel.

A NEW TRIAL IS SOUGHT

Defense Makes Motion on Ground That Justice Hitz's Charge Was Prejudicial.

Special to The New York Times.

WASHINGTON, Oct. 25.—Albert B. Fall of Three Rivers, N. M., was found guilty today of accepting, when Secretary of the Interior under President Harding, a bribe of $100,000 from Edward L. Doheny, the Los Angeles oil operator, in consideration for this bribe, the government charged, Mr. Fall leased to Mr. Doheny the Elk Hills naval oil reserve in Southern California.

Mr. Fall faces a prison sentence. American Cabinet to be adjudged a felon by a jury of his fellow-citizens.

Under Section 117 of the Criminal Code, Fall may be sent to prison for not exceeding three years, or fined three times the amount of the bribe charged, or both. A maximum punishment of that kind would be, in this instance the fine would be, if the maximum were imposed, $300,000.

In addition, the law provides that a public official convicted of bribery shall be forever disqualified from holding public office or other positions

TWO SAY THEY TOOK $63,000 TO WARDER, $20,000 TO HIS WIFE

Dell 'Osso Testifies to Five More Trips With Cash to Former Banking Official.

SAW FERRARI ON HIS KNEES

Asserts He Found President of City Trust Pleading With Defendant.

LABATE ON THE STAND

Declares He Delivered Money to Mrs. Warder—State Seeks to Submit Apartment Lease.

Delivery of $63,000 in large bills from Francesco M. Ferrari, president of the City Trust Company, to Frank H. Warder, president of banks, was testified to yesterday by Lamberto Dell' Osso at Mr. Warder's trial for accepting a bribe to withhold an examination of the tottering bank.

Dell' Osso, brother-in-law of the late Mr. Ferrari, also told Justice Arthur S. Tompkins and a jury that he had to deal with Dell' Osso pleading with the bank superintendent.

J. Vincent Labate testified he brought $20,000 to the Warder home and delivered it to Mrs. Warder. With the $10,000 Dell' Osso told about on Thursday, the prosecution has brought the total of bribes to $93,000 in alleged bribes. There has been testimony also of the delivery of sealed envelopes from Ferrari to Warder.

Tells of Five Trips to Warder Home.

Dell' Osso was a stolid witness despite his lack of facility with the

STOCKS GAIN AS MARKET IS STEADIED; BANKERS PLEDGE CONTINUED SUPPORT; HOOVER SAYS BUSINESS BASIS IS SOUND

President Hoover Issues a Statement of Reassurance On Continued Prosperity of Fundamental Business

Special to The New York Times.

WASHINGTON, Oct. 25.—A reassuring statement that the fundamental business of the country was on a sound and prosperous basis was made by President Hoover at the White House this afternoon. It was made in reply to questions by newspaper men asking his opinion on the possible effect on the nation's prosperity of yesterday's collapse in the stock market.

So far as the President is concerned, he is understood to have received detailed reports of the break in securities values, and of the current activities of the country's industries, from Secretary Mellon and other officials at the Cabinet meeting this morning.

The text of his statement headed, "In reply to press question as to the business situation, the President said," was as follows:

The fundamental business of the country, that is production and distribution of commodities, is on a sound and prosperous basis. The best evidence is that although production and consumption are at high levels, the average price of commodities as a whole have not increased and there have been no appreciable increases in the stocks of manufactured goods. Moreover, there has been a tendency of wages to increase and the output per worker in many industries again shows an increase, all of which indicates a healthy condition.

The construction and building material industries have been to some extent affected by the high interest rates induced by stock speculation and there has been some seasonal decrease in one or two other industries, but these movements are of secondary character when considered in the whole situation.

A temporary drop in grain prices sympathetically with Stock Exchange prices usually happens, but as the Department of Agriculture points out, the world price of grain is that of last year's crop and is stabilized, as it is estimated to be, 500,000,000 bushels greater than that of last year, which will result in a very low carryover at the end of the harvest year.

URGE A NEW PARK AV. BUILT ABOVE TRACKS FROM 96TH ST. NORTH

Mayor's Traffic Advisers Ask Decking Over of Viaduct to Both Building Lines.

PREDICT BIG REALTY GAINS

Avenue at a Height of Four Stories Would Have Garages and Storage Area Beneath.

PROMPT ACTION PROPOSED

Negotiation With Central Necessary. Day & Zimmerman, Point Out— Bridge Feeders Favored.

The decking-over of Park Avenue above the level of the New York Central viaduct from Ninety-sixth Street to a point just south of the Harlem River to create a new through-travel artery at a maximum height of four stories above the present street level was the recommendation made to the Merchant-Zimmerman traffic survey report submitted to Mayor Walker and the Board of Estimate on Thursday. The report recommends that such a project be started as soon as possible and be completed. The construction will result in the construction north of Ninety-sixth Street of the same high class of structures as now flank Park Avenue south of that point.

The report suggests that the new highway, to be created by decking over the present street to a height of about four stories above the railroad tracks below. The four stories below the level of the new highway, it was suggested, could be used for basement storage, garages and kitchens beneath the need for space underneath the railroad tracks, would

TRADING IS NEAR NORMAL

5,923,220 Shares Are Sold—Fluctuations in Price Narrow.

BAKER JOINS BANKING POOL

Strong Coalition to Protect Values Restores Confidence and Halts Liquidation.

OFFICIALS ARE OPTIMISTIC

Federal Summaries Say Trade Level Is Above 1928 Mark

—Other Markets Recover.

Order came quickly out of chaos in Wall Street yesterday. Heartened by the assertion of the leading bankers and industrialists that the financial and industrial structure of the country is fundamentally sound and continued to fluctuate steady and continued to fluctuate narrowly, but evenly, throughout a trading day not far from normal.

Two developments stood out most prominently and more than any other held the attention of the country. The eyes of which were focused yesterday morning on the New York Stock Exchange. One was the remarkable stability of the prices of leading securities, after their tremendous declines of the previous

WALKER OPENS WORK ON TRIBOROUGH SPAN

FOOD CONCERNS UNITE IN $125,000,000 DEAL

With Silver - Plated Pick and National City Company Brings

Cousin of Rockefeller Jr. Gets License to Fly His Own Plane

Special to The New York Times.

ROOSEVELT FIELD, L. I., Oct. 25.—After a short period of flight training at the flying school attached to this field, J. W. Rockefeller Jr., a cousin of John D. Rockefeller Jr., was examined by the local representative of the Department of Commerce and was granted a pilot's license, it became known to him. The young pilot lives at 125 West Twelfth Street, Manhattan, has been in training for several months under F. Ray Coll man at Field Unit No. 1, and is shortly expected to purchase his own plane, which he will fly from his own plane.

Mr. Rockefeller's family is said to have heartily endorsed his flying activities.

Wreath From Hoover to Be Put On Roosevelt Grave Tomorrow

Acting as the representative of President Hoover, Brig. Gen. Hugh A. Drum, commanding the Second Army, will place on the grave of Theodore Roosevelt, at Oyster Bay, a wreath forwarded from Washington by the President. It will be the President's personal tribute to the memory of Roosevelt, whose seventy-first birthday anniversary is tomorrow.

The wreath reached the quarters of Major Gen. Hanson E. Ely, at Second Army Corps Area headquarters on Governors Island, yesterday, with instructions from President Hoover that an officer be designated to place it on the grave. General Ely at once named General Drum.

THOMAS REVEALS 1924 SCHOOL SURVEY

Charges Walker Has Ignored Findings of Committee Which City Has Not Yet Published.

CITES ATTACK ON GOMPERT

Says 'Inexperienced' Architect Was Retained—Study Pointed to Building Waste.

Norman Thomas, Socialist candidate for Mayor, made public yesterday what he said was a long-suppressed report on school construction prepared by the Cooperative and Constructive School Survey in 1924 and still unpublished by the Board of Education.

The committee's series of reports, copies of which are being printed now, and Joseph Miller Jr., secretary of the board, said that 2,000 printed copies would

REPUBLICANS TO WAR ON REBELS IN SENATE

Selection of Kahn as Treasurer of Senatorial Committee Seen as First Campaign Move.

HUSTON ENLISTED BANKER

Announcement Made at Dinner Here at Which Speakers Criticized Progressive Group.

Otto H. Kahn, partner in the banking firm of Kuhn, Loeb & Co., has been selected the treasurership of the Republican Senatorial Campaign Committee, at the request of Senator George H. Moses of New Hampshire, chairman of the committee, and Claudius H. Huston, the new chairman of the Republican National Committee, it was learned yesterday.

City's Commerce—Praise the Mayor's Administration.

War on Progressives Seen

Report Ignored, Says Thomas.

Doheny Curses Court.

Fall Warned to Keep Nerve.

Critidize Insurgent Group.

General Electric and Westinghouse Join R.C.A.-Victor Corporation Radio Merger

By The Associated Press.

CAMDEN, N. J., Oct. 28.—Camden was designated tonight as a manufacturing and distributing center for the home entertainment devices of the Radio-Victor Company and the Westinghouse Electric and the Westinghouse companies which have ceded to the R. C. A.-Victor Corporation all rights in apparatus and patents.

Price Fluctuations Are Narrow.

Prices Higher at Opening.

Stock Basis Agreed Upon.

Urge Triborough Bridge Spur.

Walker Administration Praised.

Witness Mutters as He Nerves.

La Guardia Lost Chance to Meet Party Chiefs As Aide in Error Declined Huston Dinner Bid

Tells Present Procedure.

Continued on Page Five.
Continued on Page Fourteen.
Continued on Page Three.

The New York Times.

"All the News That's Fit to Print." ★★★★

VOL. LXXIX....No. 26,211.

Copyright, 1929, by The New York Times Company.

NEW YORK, TUESDAY, OCTOBER 29, 1929.

TWO CENTS In Greater New York | FOUR CENTS Elsewhere Within 200 Miles | Except 7th and 8th Postal Zones

THE WEATHER

Rain today and probably tomorrow; somewhat colder tomorrow.

Temperatures Yesterday—Max., 62; Min., 47.
☞ Full Weather Report on Page 32.

STOCK PRICES SLUMP $14,000,000,000 IN NATION-WIDE STAMPEDE TO UNLOAD; BANKERS TO SUPPORT MARKET TODAY

Sixteen Leading Issues Down $2,893,520,108; Tel. & Tel. and Steel Among Heaviest Losers

A shrinkage of $2,893,520,108 in the open market value of the shares of sixteen representative companies resulted from yesterday's sweeping decline on the New York Stock Exchange.

American Telephone and Telegraph was the heaviest loser. $448,905,162 having been lopped off of its total value. United States Steel common, traditional bellwether of the stock market, made its greatest nose-dive in recent years by falling from a high of 202⅜ to a low of 185. In a feeble last-minute rally it snapped back to 186, at which it closed, showing a net loss of 17⅜ points. This represented for the 8,131,055 shares of common stock outstanding a total loss in value of $142,293,446.

In the following table are shown the day's net depreciation in the outstanding shares of the sixteen companies referred to:

Issues.	Shares Listed.	Depreciation. Points.	Depreciation.
American Radiator	10,096,289	10%	$104,748,997
American Tel. & Tel.	13,208,093	34	448,905,162
Commonwealth & Southern	30,764,488	3	96,138,962
Columbia Gas & Electric	6,477,307	23	156,380,734
Consolidated Gas	11,651,188	20	229,023,760
DuPont E. I.	10,322,481	14½	149,030,626
Eastman Kodak	2,239,703	41½	93,868,813
General Electric	7,211,494	47½	342,545,460
General Motors	43,500,000	6½	293,625,000
International Nickel	13,777,408	7½	108,497,068
New York Central	4,507,086	22¾	104,916,071
Radio Corporation	24,843,642	7	174,615,460
Standard Oil of New Jersey	8,720,173	20	142,293,446
United States Steel	8,131,055	17⅜	142,293,446
United Gas Improvement	18,646,835	4¾	88,580,986
Westinghouse Elec. & Mfg.	2,399,265	34½	82,682,326
			$2,893,520,108

The stocks included in the foregoing table are typical, but include only a few of the "blue chips" that fell widely. Some of the medium-priced stocks were swept down almost as sharply as the "big stocks." The loss in open-market value by General Motors, for instance, was greater than that of some of the higher priced issues such as Consolidated Gas and New York Central.

For some of the market's trading favorites yesterday was the most disastrous day since they were admitted to trading.

PREMIER ISSUES HARD HIT

Unexpected Torrent of Liquidation Again Rocks Markets.

DAY'S SALES 9,212,800

Nearly 3,000,000 Shares Are Traded In Final Hour—The Tickers Lag 167 Minutes.

NEW RALLY SOON BROKEN

Selling by Europeans and "Mob Psychology" Big Factors in Second Big Break.

The second hurricane of liquidation within four days hit the stock market yesterday. It came suddenly and violently, after holders of stocks had been lulled into a sense of security by the rallies of Friday and Saturday. It was a country-wide collapse of open-market security values in the record-breaking transactions of the Stock Exchange. The collapse of the actual losses taken in dollars and cents were, probably the most disastrous and far-reaching in the history of the Stock Exchange.

That the storm has now blown itself out, that there will be organized support to absorb the present supply of stocks and that the market has passed, at least for the time being, the worst reaction which has ripped billions of dollars...

EUROPE IS DISTURBED BY AMERICAN ACTION ON OCCUPATION DEBT

London Urges an Explanation of Move for Direct Payments by Germany.

BANK'S PRESTIGE INVOLVED

Britain and Continent Feel That We Do Not Have Faith in Young Plan Institution.

By EDWIN L. JAMES.
Special Cable to The New York Times.

LONDON, Oct. 28.—There appears to exist in London a certain amount of misunderstanding of the significance of the conversations between Washington and Berlin which now concerns the ripen into diplomatic negotiations in the German capital for the preparation of a treaty dealing with the future funding of the Reich's to United States to cover costs of the army of occupation. It seems the French capital shares with London the lack of appreciation of the means by...

America's debt to the United States for occupation costs has been figured as part of the Dawes reparations debt. This was true in drafting the Dawes plan and also in writing the Young plan. Under the Young plan occupation costs were reckoned at $2,000,000 marks (about $24,000,000) annually and during the Washington committee negotiations of the...

SCHEME IS LAID TO HOOVER

President Is Said to Wish to Avoid Clash in Congress Over Linking of Reparations and War Debts.

SENATOR T. E. BURTON, LONG ILL, DIES AT 77

Ohio Statesman Had Served in Congress for 41 Years—First Elected to the House.

STRONG ADVOCATE OF PEACE

Was Among Early Hoover Supporters.—President Visited Him in Last Illness at Capital.

Special to The New York Times.
WASHINGTON, Oct. 28.—Senator Theodore E. Burton of Ohio died tonight at 9:50. He had been ill since last Friday, which was the last time he was able to attend a session of the Senate. At 9:45 his night nurse noted that Senator Burton's temperature was rising and his pulse, until then strong and regular, had become irregular...

Roosevelt's Memory Honored In Navy Day Fete on Ships

Ships at sea and in port officially celebrated Navy Day yesterday. Although major land celebrations were held on Sunday, the anniversary of the birth of Theodore Roosevelt, who established Navy Day, aboard ships were reserved for yesterday.

Open house was kept by ships in the port while the public was invited to visit them. Flags appropriate for the day were broken out on all government ships, and even some commercial craft in the harbor here flew pennants in honor of the navy.

The Los Angeles and the new airship dirigible and other lighter-than-air craft at Lakehurst, N. J., were ordered out and cruised north along the Atlantic coast, passing over this city and Long Island.

BINGHAM ACCUSES SENATORS OF PLOT TO BESMIRCH HIM; NORRIS TO ASK FOR CENSURE

Johnson and Harrison Call for His Guidance as Chamber Clashes Over Bill's Fate.

CONFERENCE DEMISE SEEN

Accusing Republicans of This Aim, Simmons Holds President Responsible With Party.

SMOOT ISSUES CHALLENGE

He Denies "Killing Plan" and Pleads for Passage.—Robinson Pledges Democratic Aid in Speeding It.

Special to The New York Times.
WASHINGTON, Oct. 28.—During a debate which amply illustrating the nervousness of the Senate over the tariff bill today. President Hoover was again called upon to put the bill into the position on the duties on agricultural and industrial products.

This demand, made by Senators Johnson, Republican, of California, and Harrison, Democrat, of Mississippi, was rejected when Senator Johnson sought definite information on President Reed's Saturday night statement in Philadelphia that the bill was "dead."...

SENATORS RENEW DEMAND ON HOOVER FOR TARIFF STAND

BINGHAM'S ATTACK BITTER

Charges Lobby Inquiry With Throwing at Him 'Political Slime.'

CALLS ITS METHODS UNFAIR

Caraway Asking Those to Stand Who Approve Eyanson Episode, Gets No Response.

OTHER MEMBERS HIT BACK

Norris Will Draw Up Resolution Against Connecticut Senator for Presentation Today.

Special to The New York Times.
WASHINGTON, Oct. 28.—Senator Hiram Bingham of Connecticut bitterly attacked in the Senate today the lobby investigating committee, which had shown that he had employed an official of the Connecticut Manufacturers' Association as his tariff adviser, and drew, in turn, from the four members active in its committee's work, a series of vigorous assaults on his course...

Robot to Guide Airplane, Relieving Strain on Pilot

Special to The New York Times.
WASHINGTON, Oct. 28.—A robot airplane pilot which, it is claimed, will automatically stabilize a plane on the lateral, longitudinal and vertical axes, has been patented in Germany by a Berlin company, according to information received by the Department of Commerce...

KAROLYIS GET RIGHT TO ENTER COUNTRY

Stimson Raises Ban Against Hungarian Count and Countess Placed by Hughes in 1925.

LIBERAL POLICY IS SEEN

Secretary, Granting Visa, Says Department in Past Acted on Political Ground.

SEEN NEAR MOUNT TAYLOR

One of Passengers on Craft Bound East is W. E. Merz of Mount Vernon.

Continued on Page Seven.

INVESTMENT TRUSTS TO AID

Financiers at Meeting Agree Prices Are Now More Attractive and Money Is Plentiful.

Market Leaders Hard Hit.

Orderly Market's Aim.

Continued on Page Twenty-one.

Architects Picked to Plan Rockefeller Centre, Which May Have Opera House as a Nucleus

Burial to Be in Cleveland.

Elected to House in 1886.

Continued on Page Twenty-four.

City Traffic Lights Now Blink 20 Hours a Day; Whalen Also Cuts Intervals to Speed Vehicles

Would Pass Through Bank.

MacDonald Sent Message.

Body to Lie in State.

Johnson Asks Bill's Chances.

Continued on Page Eighteen.

Charges Committee Was "Packed."

Indicates More Liberal Policy.

Bingham Addresses the Senate.

Continued on Page Twenty-five.

4
Eighteenth-Century Foreign Panics

The uninitiated tend to forget
that a monetary system is
basically a regulating device.
Jacques Rueff

TWO OF the best-known panics of the pre-twentieth-century era are foreign panics, one French and one British. They were staged with grandeur and fell with equal grandeur. The French (with the exception of the assignat crisis of the 1790s) and the British have never seen panics of this magnitude since. Perhaps they learned a lesson for all time. Because Americans have never felt such dramatic collapses, we may in our smugness get a little careless. Therefore I relate these two granddaddies of all panics, in order that we might learn from the mistakes of OTHERS.

THE SOUTH SEA BUBBLE

Try to put yourself back at the beginning of the eighteenth century in England. It was a great time. London was the bustling center of the world. England was master of Europe. Its citizens were enjoying the good things of life. Everywhere men were living and spending lavishly. Trade was booming. And money — lots of it — was floating around.

A great construction boom had developed and promoters in this field were raking it in. It was a "get rich quick" atmosphere, not unlike that in America in the 1920s or, for that matter, in the 1960s when the 28-year-old hotshot gunslinger managers of "growth funds" were promising a pie in the sky to Americans who had money burning a hole in their pockets.

In the early 1700s in England there had not yet developed a multiplicity of corporations in which one could invest. In fact, the London "Big Board" of that time was dominated by just three major finan-

cial corporations — the Bank of England, the East
India Company, and the South Sea Company. The
bank is still with us. The East India Company is
known to all of us from our school days as that great
enterprise which promoted the development of the
Indian subcontinent, and made a bundle in the process. The South Sea Company is probably less well
known, for it was a comet which shot across the skies
for the brief period of ten years at the beginning of
the 1700s, then disappeared into nothingness. But in
the process of its short history it created so much
trouble that it almost brought England to its financial knees.

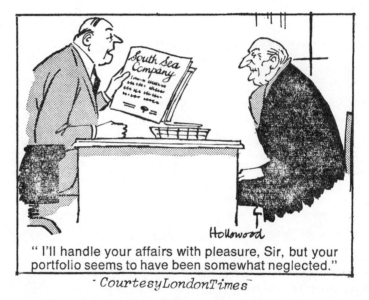

" I'll handle your affairs with pleasure, Sir, but your
portfolio seems to have been somewhat neglected."

- *CourtesyLondonTimes*

The South Sea Company received its royal
charter in 1711. And the king himself — George I —
was its governor. The commercial basis for the company was a monopoly to trade in the South Seas, and
this embraced a very large area, ranging from all of
South America to the west coast of North America,
and from all beyond to the West where the bounda-

ries of its monopoly met those of the East India Company in the Far East.This, obviously, was a commercial and financial plum of the very first order. For it was Britain who ruled the seas of the world. Its military and commercial power stood unchallenged.

Despite these glowing commercial prospects, the company got off to a rather inauspicious start financially.

In a rather high-handed maneuver, the holders of £9.5 million of government debts were forced to exchange these securities for stock in the new company. And at par. Well, that's one way of doing an underwriting, but hardly one that would be acceptable today. Initially, these investors were not very happy, for the stock sank from par to 77½ only two months after the deal was put together. For years thereafter, it showed no better performance. It soon became clear that the promoters of this scheme were not genuinely interested in its commercial potential. The investors even less so, for they, in harmony with the times, were out for a fast buck, and not interested in a process of long-term solid corporate development.

In 1719 things started to look up. In that year a wave of new speculation was sweeping the country, and the directors of the South Sea Company, sensing that the timing was right, put together a plan which would make their company the most influential corporation in all of England, and even relegate the Bank of England to second place.

In November 1719 the rather audacious plan was presented to the government. The idea was to pay off the national debt — all of it (remember these were still the "good old days") — by incorporating it with the stock of the South Sea Company. Involved was £51,300,000. From the government's standpoint, this represented a terrific deal. For this debt had originally been contracted when interest rates were sky-high. The South Sea Company offered to take over the entire debt in return for an annual payment of only 5 percent interest, which was even to be reduced to 4 percent after 1727. On top of offering such beneficial rates, the South Sea Company immediately offered to pay the government £3.5 million "for the privilege of taking over the debt."

The proposal was introduced to the House of Commons on January 22, 1720, with the assurance that, if accepted, it would completely eradicate the public debt in twenty-five years. On the other hand, whispers and rumors abounded to the effect that prominent politicians and courtiers were purchasing stock. In fact, Mr. Aislabie, the nation's treasurer, was supposed to have bought £27,000 worth of it himself. In view of this, a member of the opposite party (the Whigs) suggested that since this entire transaction appeared to be beneficial to only a chosen few (its promoters in the South Sea Company), the deal should be thrown open to a public bid. The House of Commons agreed with this proposal, and, with visible chagrin, our friend Mr. Aislabie was compelled to agree to receive further proposals.

The Bank of England, which saw that its key role in British financial affairs was in great danger, immediately came through with an offer of £5 million for the same "privileges." Whereupon the directors of the South Sea Company went one up, and made an offer of £7,567,000. They won.

It is rather difficult for us today even to imagine such a transaction. In our current context, this would mean that some U.S. corporation would make a bid for the $300 billion federal debt, and throw in $50 billion as a kicker. These are things that a Mr.

Ling, or even a Mr. Cornfeld, would never have thought about, even in their wildest dreams. To be sure, "only" £50 million was involved, but in dealing with the early eighteenth century, one must avoid thinking in terms of today's values or today's exchange rates. At that time, £50 million represented a good portion of the *total* money in circulation.

What did the directors of the South Sea Company expect to get from this highly unusual transaction? Really nothing more than the opportunity to catch the public eye in an unprecedented fashion, as the world's first superconglomerate, and then "go public" by issuing treasury stock at a great premium. In other words, they were to set a pattern which was to be followed by countless numbers of promoters since.

This then was the whole basis of the story of the "bubble" which would go down in history. The South Sea Company was duly authorized to create £1 of new stock for every £1 of debt it had taken over from the government. The next step was to take these newly created shares to the market. The directors were highly optimistic about the success of their public offering, and foresaw that they could immediately raise the funds to pay the multi-million-pound kicker to the British government, and still have a lot left over to make profits and cover a further item of expense which had, unfortunately, been necessary to get this venture off the ground, namely, a whole series of bribes which had been given to prominent politicians and courtiers, including even the royal mistress. In a way, eighteenth-century England was really not that much different from twentieth-century Latin America or Italy. (Some might even add Chicago.)

As it turned out the directors of the South Sea

Company had played their cards extremely well. The shares of the South Sea Company which had been quoted at 128½ on January 1, 1720 (already very nicely over par), were going for 330 by the end of March. With the price so nicely run up, the corporation officers struck. They opened up a subscription for new stock in the company on April 14, and it was immediately heavily oversubscribed. Well over £2 million came in at 300.

So far so good.

But the whole scheme stood or fell with the company's being able to generate a large and continuing inflow of funds from the investing public. So the South Sea promoters came up with another brilliant idea. In order to furnish the market with funds for fresh buying of their stock, and to offer a new incentive, the company offered to loan money against stock deposited on what was called "the installment plan." Sound familiar? Each £100 of South Sea stock entitled its depositors to a loan of £250 at 5 percent interest.

So successful was this new gimmick that it was repeated no less than three times. This was possible as a result of still another ploy by the company's directors, which ploy insured that the money they lent would, for the most part, come back to the company in the form of new stock subscriptions. The objective of this new exercise was to eliminate the competition for such investable funds.

For, all of a sudden, competition had appeared from all sides. London, being then as now a city full of clever people in the financial field, was stunned by the success of the South Sea Company, and thus it immediately brought forth hundreds of similar schemes. A true rage for stock brokerage sprang up simultaneously, and the overall result was a transformation, almost overnight, of English society. The expansion of credit and the rise of speculation went hand in hand. One acute observer of these times, Edward Harley the younger, described the situation in February 1720: "There are few in London that mind anything but the rising and falling of the stock."

This is what had happened: regardless of legal restrictions which normally made it extremely difficult to form new companies, new "joint stock schemes" (in other words, companies based upon publicly owned shares), usually bought on credit, sprang up every day. Probably this was the beginning of the over-the-counter market. Then, as today, "cats and dogs" abounded. Also, then, as today, many of these schemes were successfully launched not because of any real value involved, but because of the name of the man or men that fronted the projects.

The Prince of Wales had himself appointed as the governor of the Welsh Copper Company. The Duke of Bridgewater formed a company for building houses in London and Westminster. The Duke of Chandos became head of the York Building Company. By chance, all three of these schemes were genuine, but countless numbers of others, which received the name "bubbles," were not.

Many of these "bubble" schemes had lunacy written all over their faces. For instance, there was one scheme involving £1 million of newly issued stock, issued to the greedy and gullible public, "for a wheel for perpetual motion." Other promoters did not even bother to think up anything whatsoever. Thus a typical prospectus of this period announced the formation of a company "for carrying on an undertaking of great advantage" and went on to state that every subscriber "who deposits £2 per share is to be entitled to £100 per annum." Not a bad deal! Except that nobody could ever find out what this "undertaking of great advantage" was, due to the simple fact that it did not exist. But no matter. Within five hours this absurd prospectus attracted over £2,000 to its "head office" in the center of London. In the sixth hour the company "director" decamped.

It was computed that the sums which were sought to be raised by such speculative undertakings amounted to as much as £300 million.

The directors of the South Sea Company immediately recognized the danger in this. Every pound which went to share subscriptions of another company would be lost to them. And they badly needed these funds to keep their perpetual-motion financial machine going. (Reminds one of the needs of mutual funds for net inflow.)

So they went back to their friends in parliament and had the so-called Bubble Act passed. Essentially, this act made all companies illegal which had not obtained a royal charter. And these, of course, were very few and far between. The politicians and royalty whom the South Sea Company had "bought" had seen to that. This act became law on June 20, 1720, and, as a result of further arm-twisting by the South Sea fellows, the Lord Justices of England proclaimed no fewer than eighty-six "bubble" companies illegal, and put them out of existence. Actually this sort of thing was the prerogative of the king, but he was in disgrace at the moment, and had gone back to live with dad and mom in Germany. In his place, the Lord Justices had been appointed as temporary regents.

Once again this whole thing worked in favor of the South Sea Company. In the weeks that followed the passing of this new act, its shares once again rose. On July 10, the price hit 1,000.

But the people behind the South Sea Company had now gone too far. The passing and enforcing of the Bubble Act proved to be their undoing. It had started a panic!

No one knew exactly which companies would be declared illegal under this new act. Thus every company, and the shares of every company, had become suspect. Even the York Building Company, a solid and legitimate corporation, saw the price of its shares fall in half overnight, and in a few days no buyers at any price could be found.

Hundreds and hundreds of corporations found themselves in exactly the same situation. Inevitably, the fears of the times soon began to affect the South Sea Company.

Against all logic, the company tried a *fourth* flotation on the market. It failed. The news got around, and the market price of the old shares started to fall, and fall, and fall. By mid-September 1720, they were down to 400, just two months after reaching a peak of 1,000.

The directors of the company now tried a final desperate move. They announced that the company would pay a 30 percent dividend at Christmas of 1720, and that the dividend would be increased to 50 percent minimum in subsequent years. But where the money for these payments was to come from even the directors did not know. The South Sea Company had done literally nothing to develop the potential of that great territory over which it had trading monopoly. The company, in essence, had very little current income, and its expenses, especially directors' fees, were high. It was truly a bubble, which had to be expanded and expanded and expanded through new public issues of stock and ever-increasing credit — until it burst.

Seeing the writing on the wall, the officers of the South Sea Company sought a final out. They turned to their old enemy, the Bank of England, and put to it a proposal under which the bank would take over large blocks of South Sea stock at 400. This was a move that, in a sense, would recur in 1929, when the Establishment on Wall Street got together as buyers, in a last-ditch attempt to stem the flood of stock sales. But as in 1929, in 1720 it did not work either. The Bank of England refused to ratify the proposal. Its reasons were good, the bank itself was in grave trouble. Its stock, which had stood at 263 in summer, was down to 145 by the end of October. The entire system of credit in England had been brought to the brink of total collapse as company after company went under. Commercial ventures lay strewn in wreckage throughout London.

Finally the company that had started it all, the South Sea Company, went under. The last-ditch attempt to revive it, that is, bringing back the company's governor, King George I, from his German exile, also ended in failure.

An inquiry was made the following year, and the whole affair was attributed to the nefarious practices of the company's directors who were the leading members of the Establishment.

But the real causes lay in the primitive instincts of politicians in particular and people in general. Politicians, eager for power and recognition, had agreed to a harebrained scheme; instead of facing reality when it became obvious that it was doomed to failure, they agreed to one stupid measure after the other, merely postponing the evil day of collapse. They ultimately brought the whole country to the edge of financial ruin, instead of just one company.

There are no exact parallels in modern times to such political folly, but, unfortunately, we seem to be at least inching ourselves in the same direction. Take the rail industry in the United States. Or Lockheed. Instead of letting the inevitable take place, the U.S. government saw fit to prop up (with government credit) such failing enterprises, which could no longer survive on their own in a competitive society.

But in 1720 it was not just the politicians. It was the greed of speculators, trying to make something with nothing, believing that there *is* a pie in the sky. Without the willing suckers, all this would not have been possible. However, in this situation, as in every panic, there were those few hundred who made piles of money in that year. They were the ones who could sense that the whole stock boom of the time was built upon an unexplainable euphoria, and knew that when the credit bubble burst, an animal panic would break out. They coolly calculated values. They got out in June and July. They realized that the last 10 percent is never worth striving for, if one wants to preserve what one has already achieved.

Seventeen-twenty was a most memorable year for panics. For just across the channel, in France, another dandy occurred. As in England, it reached its climax in the fall of that year. So too in recent times we've had I.O.S. in Europe and Lockheed and Penn Central across the bigger channel, in the U.S. Speculation spreads. Would that wisdom were as catching.

THE MISSISSIPPI COMPANY

About one year after the South Sea Company received its charter, a Scotsman by the name of Law,

a bold and ingenious banker, was expounding ideas
to the French not far removed from our modern concepts of credit. "The workings of trade," he wrote,
"revolve wholly about money. The more you have,
the more people you can keep employed. Credit will
take the place of money and will have the same results." Law had the idea of creating apparent resources by printing money.

In 1712, the Mississippi Company was given a
monopoly to exploit the French possessions in North
America. In 1716, Law set up a General Bank to discount commercial paper. In 1718, this became the
Royal Bank, having as its sole shareholder "the
State." As backing for the bank's notes, Law used
shares in the Mississippi Company. Initially the
scheme was incredibly successful. Law advertised it
widely with flamboyant and ingenious displays: Indi-
ans bedecked with gold were paraded through Paris;
engravings were distributed showing mountains of
silver and cliffs of emeralds in Louisiana. The public
was bullish, speculation was rife, fortunes piled up
and the shares soared. "Mother shares" were split
into "daughter" and "granddaughter" shares; in order to buy "granddaughters" you had to have four
"mothers" and one "daughter."

As always, once speculation fever takes over, it
snowballs; before long people of all classes were risk-
ing their all on Law's schemes. Law sought in good
faith to recruit settlers for America and to transform
his utopia into real wealth. Unlike the directors of
the South Sea Company, his intentions were of the
best and he cannot be held to blame for the irrespon-
sible actions of speculators. The streets around the
rue Quincampoix, where the bank had its headquarters, were crammed with people. Law himself, although happily married, was much sought after by

IN LAW — Satiric engraving of 1720, by an unknown artist, depicting the famous adven-
r as a medieval alchemist. Paper bank-notes feed the fires of inflation, while sound coinage
nsumed in a vain attempt to find a magic formula for unlimited wealth. "All or nothing"
s the motto overhead as Law is presented with a worthless crown of feathers and leaves.

the social-climbing females of the era (as were all of the many personable young gentlemen who were making money with the bank) on the lookout for newly rich husbands. Law resisted the attentions of these femmes fatales valiantly, but "a duchess," wrote a princess of the era, ". . . kissed Law's hand in public. Now, if the duchesses so behave, where must not other women kiss him?"

A nation's credit, however, cannot be established upon a fluctuating basis and when the crash came, as it had to come, the system was swept away with the fools. For several months, the financiers had been bearish and suddenly panic was rife. Owners of shares and bank notes rushed the bank to get their money back. In a last-ditch effort, some of Law's highly placed friends made him controller-general and, in order to save his company, *Law immediately forbade the circulation of gold and silver.* Values continued to plunge, however, and on October 10, 1720, the Royal Bank was put out of business. Law fled to South America — a pauper.

This was not, however, merely the failure of one financier — the whole of France was shaken. The state itself had been a party to the bank. The regent had patronized it. The future regent had grown rich on it. Over one million families throughout France — not just Parisians — held the bank's notes. They had to, it was an enforced currency. The notes were not redeemed, in spite of a tremendous hue and cry at all levels of society. The rich got by; the poor got poorer. England had been strong enough to withstand the South Sea Bubble. France was not strong enough to stand the collapse of Law's systems. The monarchy tottered, and it took a hundred years and Bonaparte's genius before France was back on its feet and before anyone dared to suggest a new bank of issue.

You probably notice the great similarities between the South Sea Bubble crash and that of John Law. But the most important and fundamental similarity is that both were basically caused by an overextension of credit. This, in turn, produced a totally unreal prosperity — a "bubble," which had to burst when the laws of economics came back into force.

You can be forgiven if you shudder a little at the realization that today credit has been extended so far in the U.S.A. that the country's debt is greater than that of all the nations in the world combined. With a high credit structure, as with a knitted sweater, if you unravel just one thread at the edge, the whole thing can come unraveled. Credit vulnerability in the U.S. has never been greater.

FRENCH ASSIGNAT — The fiat paper money of the French Revolution. The overissue of this currency caused a disastrous inflation and complete breakdown of the French monetary and banking system. This 400-livre note is typical of the series begun in 1790. By 1797, after some

5

The Age of
American Socialism

A Conservative is a man with
two perfectly good legs who
has never learned to walk.
Franklin D. Roosevelt

AFTER THE disaster of 1929, government (with Franklin Delano Roosevelt at its head) took over more and more power.

As often happens at a turnaround in the business cycle, there was a complete swing in the opposite direction in politics. Gold was made illegal for private citizens to own; the Securities and Exchange Commission became the watchdog of Wall Street; various controls were set up to "stabilize" markets and the economy. The net result was a great loss of personal freedom and a depression that never really came off the bottom until World War II started, a decade later. What little progress was made in the stock market during the 1930s was erased out of what appeared to be a clear blue sky in 1937, proving that Roosevelt's "New Deal" of American-style socialism was a complete failure.

PANIC OF 1937

This was almost totally government induced. In 1936 and 1937, by stages, the Federal Reserve authorities doubled reserve requirements for member banks. However they argued that it would have no ill effects, because they were merely absorbing excess reserves. But this act alone caused a chain of reactions which resulted in increased cost of capital and weakening of the securities market. To paraphrase, their action caused money to tighten. It was only the blindness of a government which already had put so many economic "plans" into operation that made it impossible for

government leaders to realize what would happen
when they tightened money.

Added to this the Secretary of the Treasury
adopted the policy of "sterilizing" the incoming
gold in the winter of 1936–37. He did this by not issuing gold certificates against this new gold, but
instead borrowing money from commercial banks
with which to buy the gold. It meant that during
this period the gold inflow *ceased* to add to member bank reserves. Indeed it did the reverse.

Net government contribution to income was
also reduced. Government reduced the deficit, which
also tightened money. In the third quarter of 1937
there was actually an excess of cash income over
cash outflow, an event which preceded and (some
say) precipitated the crash.

As a believer in hard money and balanced
budgets I do not argue with validated methods to get
an economy back into line. But methods used here
were at best a mixture of capitalism and socialism.
However, we are not discussing the rights or wrongs
in this chapter, merely cause and effect. With any
modest awareness of the government's economic
manipulation, the Panic of 1937 was foreseeable,
when the signs of tight money appeared: that is, increased costs to borrow money, reduced profitability
of investment, and increased costs, particularly labor
costs. Then it became only a question of time before
these warning signs would have a negative effect in
the stock market.

Hence it can be said that from the investor's
viewpoint the immediate cause of the 1937 depression was a decline in the corporate profit ration and
the prospect of declines in future profits.

THE WAR YEARS

After an initial short sharp panic, based simply on the shock of America entering the war, the American economy settled down to a war boom, inflation, and controls. This trio continued throughout the war. When the war finished and war productivity tapered off, business started to stagnate. However, again the economy was "saved" by a war; the Korean War held the machinery together until 1953, though debt soared.

RECESSION OF 1953–1954

After World War II, unlike Europe, America was not plunged into a postwar depression. The main reason for this was her loan policy to war-torn Europe (that is, loaning or giving money to those who would buy U.S. goods with it), and because U.S. inflationary wartime politicies were continued, and because labor managed to negotiate wages to keep up with the inflation rate. So the whole complex was able to coast for a number of years. Then of course the Korean War added impetus to the economy, and it was only when this was all over and defense production fell that the U.S. belatedly had its recession.

Lest anyone get the idea that such unsound policies can keep a nation truly prosperous, it should be made part of the record that this postponement of problems was made possible by the following circumstances: The U.S. sold war goods to its allies during two world wars and as a result skimmed off most of their gold (the only true measure of wealth). The U.S. then proceeded to spend that gold over two

The New York Times.

VOL. LXXXII....No. 27,435.

Entered as Second-Class Matter,
Postoffice, New York, N. Y.

NEW YORK, MONDAY, MARCH 6, 1933.

Copyright, 1933, by The New York Times Company.

P

TWO CENTS In New York City. | THREE CENTS Within 200 Miles | FOUR CENTS Elsewhere Except in 7th and 8th Postal Zones

LATE CITY EDITION

WEATHER—Fair today; tomorrow cloudy, warmer, rain following
Temperatures Yesterday—Max.: 41; Min., 32.

ROOSEVELT ORDERS 4-DAY BANK HOLIDAY, PUTS EMBARGO ON GOLD, CALLS CONGRESS

HITLER BLOC WINS A REICH MAJORITY, RULES IN PRUSSIA

Stay-at-Homes Turn Out and Give Government 52% of 39,000,000 Record Vote.

NAZIS ROLL UP 17,300,000

Get 44% of Total Poll and Even Wrest the Control of Bavaria From Catholics.

ELECTION IS PEACEFUL

Berlin Is Closely Guarded—The Stahlheim Holds Parade Under Sunny Skies.

By FREDERICK T. BIRCHALL.
Special Cable to THE NEW YORK TIMES.

BERLIN, Monday, March 6.—With almost mathematical precision the results in yesterday's German elections for the Reichstag and the Prussian Diet bear out the predictions based on the pre-election campaign. Just as two and two make four, so suppression and intimidation have produced a Nationalist triumph. The rest of

---

*Mob Attacked Stalin's Home
In Wide Revolt, Tokyo Hears*

WIRELESS TO THE NEW YORK TIMES.
TOKYO, Monday, March 6.—Private information reaching Tokyo states that discontent due to famine conditions is so acute in Soviet Russia that a mob attacked Joseph Stalin's house in Moscow on Jan. 20 and was driven off. Several persons, it is reported, were killed. Other reports from Siberia, partly corroborated by information reaching military circles here, indicate the farmers are in widespread revolt. Serious disturbances occurred at Irkutsk, and 80,000 men are said to have joined the revolt, including Communists and the peasantry.

The Japanese discount a good part of these rumors, but they come from too many sources to be entirely ignored. It is believed these disturbances are much more serious than the Soviet Government has admitted.

JAPANESE PUSH ON IN FIERCE FIGHTING; CHINA CLOSES WALL

Jehol Forces Offer Stoutest Resistance of Campaign as They Are Cornered.

BUT LOSE ANOTHER PASS

Chang's Troops at Kupei Bar Retreat Southward to the Peiping Area.

NANKING ADMITS DEFEAT

Asserts 'What Will Happen Next Depends on Military'—Tientsin Fears Clashes.

By The Associated Press.

TOKYO, March 5.—Rengo (Japanese) agency dispatches from Chengteh (Jehol City) today said the final phase of the Japanese Jehol drive was underway to seize passes in the Great Wall north and northeast of Peiping, was producing some of the most bitter fighting of the whole drive. Cornered Chinese units were resisting desperately.

The Sixteenth Infantry Brigade of Major Gen. Tadashi Kawahara, in

---

CERMAK NEAR END; LAPSES INTO COMA

Death Is Imminent From Shot Aimed by Zangara at Roosevelt.

FAMILY AT HIS 'BEDSIDE

Third Transfusion Futile in

---

*Relief Wages Will Be Paid
Despite Holiday, Gibson Says*

Harvey D. Gibson, chairman of the Emergency Unemployment Relief Committee, declared yesterday that the bank holiday would not interfere with the payment of wages to unemployed men and women holding emergency jobs through the committee's work and relief bureau.

"Emergency wages must be paid and some way must be found to pay them," he said. "There is no doubt that we will find a way to do it. We are not worried about it at all. Arrangements can certainly be made to meet the emergency relief payroll."

The weekly payroll of the committee exceeds $1,000,000.

BANKS HERE ACT AT ONCE

City Scrip to Be Ready Today or Tomorrow to Replace Currency.

EMERGENCY STEP PRAISED

Financiers Look for Little Interruption in Business Under Federal Program.

'TRUST DEPOSITS' TO AID

Cash Now Can Be Placed in New Accounts and Drawn Upon Without Limitation.

Clearing House certificates will be issued in New York, if needed, just as soon as they are printed, possibly today and probably tomorrow. Meanwhile, as a result of President Roosevelt's proclamation of last night.

The President's emergency decree not only made the banking holiday national and extended it through Thursday when Congress meets in special session, but it also gave the banks permission to issue scrip in the form of Clearing House certificates to take the place of regular currency.

Thus there will be little or no in-

BEWILDERED CITY STILL PAYS IN CASH

Faces Use of Scrip Calmly and Continues to Patronize the Theatres and Stores.

HOPEFUL MOOD PREVAILS

Merchants and Travel Lines Uncertain on Use of Tender—Many Extending Credit.

Bewildered but still cheerful, the

The President's Bank Proclamation

USE OF SCRIP AUTHORIZED

President Takes Steps Under Sweeping Law of War Time.

PRISON FOR GOLD HOARDER

The Proclamation Provides for Withdrawals From Banks Against New Deposits.

CONGRESS SITS THURSDAY

Day of Conference With the Cabinet and Financial Men Precedes the Decree.

Special to THE NEW YORK TIMES.

WASHINGTON, March 5.—The text of President Roosevelt's proclamation on the banking situation, issued at the White House at 11 o'clock tonight, was as follows:

BY THE PRESIDENT OF THE UNITED STATES OF AMERICA.

A Proclamation

WHEREAS there have been heavy and unwarranted withdrawals of gold and currency from our banking institutions for the purpose of hoarding; and

WHEREAS continuous and increasingly extensive speculative activity abroad in foreign exchange has resulted in severe drains on the nation's stocks of gold; and

WHEREAS these conditions have created a national emergency; and

WHEREAS it is in the best interests of all bank depositors that a period of respite be provided with a view to preventing further hoarding of coin, bullion or currency or speculation in foreign exchange and permitting the application of appropriate measures to protect the interests of our people; and

WHEREAS it is provided in Section 5 (b) of the act of Oct. 6, 1917 (40 Stat. L. 411) as amended, "that the President may investigate, regulate, or prohibit, under such rules and regulations as he may prescribe, by means of licenses or otherwise, any transactions in foreign exchange and the export, hoarding, melting or earmarkings of gold or silver coin or bullion or currency * * *";

WHEREAS it is provided in Section 16 of the said act "that whoever shall wilfully violate any of the provisions of this act or of any license, rule or regulation issued thereunder, and any person who shall wilfully violate, neglect or refuse to comply with any order of the President issued in compliance with the provisions of this act, shall, upon conviction, be fined not more than $10,000 or, if a natural person, imprisoned for not more than ten years or both * * *";

NOW, THEREFORE, I, FRANKLIN D. ROOSEVELT, PRESIDENT OF THE UNITED STATES OF AMERICA, IN VIEW OF SUCH NATIONAL EMERGENCY AND BY VIRTUE of the authority vested in me by said act and in order to prevent the export, hoarding or earmarking of gold or silver coin or bullion or currency, do hereby proclaim, order, direct and declare that from Monday, the sixth day of March, to Thursday, the ninth day of March, nineteen hundred and thirty-three, both dates inclusive, there shall be maintained and observed by all banking institutions

---

Special to THE NEW YORK TIMES.

WASHINGTON, March 5.—To prevent the export, hoarding or earmarking of gold or silver, coin or bullion or currency, President Roosevelt issued a proclamation at 11 o'clock tonight, in which by order dered a bank holiday from tomorrow through Thursday, March 9. Earlier in the day he had summoned a special session of Congress to meet on Thursday.

This sweeping action was taken after a day of conference, among officials and bankers, the President taking recourse to war powers granted under the trading-with-the-

ON GOLD STANDARD, WOODIN DECLARES

Other High Officials Concur in His View of Suspending Payments for Period.

Conference Will Centre on Bank Problem—Confidence in President Apparent.

Special to The New York Times.

WASHINGTON, March 5.—Secretary of the Treasury William H. Woodin declared tonight emphatically that the United States had not gone off the gold standard in account of the proclamation of the President. He was supported in this view by other high officials of the administration, both in the immediate issue of banking moratoriums, with the possibility that actual Federal action to be suggested by President Roosevelt.

Secretary Woodin said:

"It is ridiculous and misleading to say that we have gone off the gold standard, any more than the issue in originally calling the currency standard. We have become entirely secondary. It is just that everyone can withdraw gold merely because it can be obtained for several years in other

Continued on Page Six.

In order that there may not be a complete suspension of all banking and exchange operations, the proclamation authorizes the issuance of scrip, which may be used as currency until the banks return to more normal functioning.

Points of the Proclamation.

The main points in the proclamation are:

1. A national banking holiday from March 6 to March 9 inclusive.

An embargo on the withdrawal of gold and silver for export or domestic use during that period, except with permission of the Secretary of the Treasury.

...

IN WITNESS WHEREOF I have hereunto set my hand and caused the seal of the United States to be affixed.

Done in the City of Washington this 6th day of March, 1 A. M., in the year of Our Lord One Thousand Nine Hundred and Thirty-three, and of the Independence of the United States the one hundred and fifty-seventh.

FRANKLIN D. ROOSEVELT.

By the President:
CORDELL HULL,
Secretary of State.

(SEAL)

Continued on Page Three.

Continued on Page Three.

Continued on Page Three.

Continued on Page Eight.

Continued on Page Fourteen.

decades like a profligate nephew of a rich uncle who
died. The inheritance was totally spent. All U.S. gold
is now either gone or mortgaged three times over. But
the spending gave the illusion of prosperity and
wealth. Now only debt remains where once there
was gold, owned free and clear. Economies can be
made to linger longer without normal and healthy
correction only at grim cost to the future and at a
current cost of currency debasement and moral debasement as well — because history over thousands
of years shows that currency corruption leads to
equal degradation of the people of that civilization.
But enough of economic philosophy. Let's get back to
our story.

Apart from the fall in defense production this
recession was also brought about by the policy of
dear money which was instituted in the spring of
1953. However, most of the fall in inventory investment in the 15 months after mid-1953 was a direct
result of falling defense output, causing a reduction
in work, and in the stocks of materials of companies
making armaments.

In the words of the President's Economic Report of 1954:

> The restrictive monetary and debt manage-
> ment policies pursued in the early months of
> the year had . . . a more potent effect than was
> generally expected. . . . The demand for credit
> that developed in May and June was not,
> therefore, confined to the funds needed for
> current operations. . . . Some lenders became
> reluctant to commit funds for future use. . . .
> The Federal Reserve authorities responded to
> the incipient, and possibly dangerous, scram-

ble for liquidity with a degree of promptness and vigor for which there is no close parallel in our central bank history.

Hence it can be said that the significant features of the 1953–54 recession are the role of falling defense output, the use of federal fiscal policy in sustaining personal income, and the changes in monetary policy. Government was clearly alpha and omega. The private sector was well on the way to becoming a minority — as it already is in some nations.

1957–58 RECESSION

The end of the boom in 1957 and the recession in 1958 were brought on by two major influences. First and most important was the natural ending of the fixed-investment boom. By the second half of 1956 planned capacity equalled desired capacity. New orders placed with equipment manufacturers declined from the end of 1956. Production of equipment started to decline in the second quarter of 1956; shipments fell in the final quarter. The second influence was the fall in defense production. Since 1953 the ordering and output of defense goods had fluctuated. Output rose to a peak in 1955 and declined thereafter. There was also a fall in exports to the British, Canadian, and Japanese markets. In October 1957 the Federal Reserve adopted a dear money policy, the main effect being to delay the revival of housing starts.

1962 PANIC

By the end of the 1950s the U.S. started to lose gold on a really large scale. The immediate cause of the loss in 1958–59 was a large deficit on current account, a rapid rise in imports, together with a decline in exports as Western European countries experienced a brief recession. The situation became worse in 1960.

Higher interest rates abroad in the middle of the year caused an outflow of short term funds, and this outflow increased with a loss of confidence in the dollar and a rise in the price of gold in London late in the year. The problem was aggravated by the unwillingness of the monetary authorities to raise interest rates. At the end of the year *de facto* confidence was restored via presidential declarations and a number of administrative measures to economize in the use of foreign exchange. This time extension of "prosperity" was purchased by President Kennedy by further reduction of individual liberty — especially with regard to exchange controls. The citizen lost more of his ability to contain his governors. Another recession causative factor was the steel strike of 1959. It lasted 116 days. It was anticipated in advance and inventories were stockpiled. These high levels of activity were among the influences which created the inflationary pressures and fears which led U.S. monetary authorities to raise rates and restrict credit. Another factor was the anti-inflationary federal monetary and fiscal policy. Federal Reserve discount rates were raised in March and again in May 1959. Between January 1960 and January 1961 production of durable goods fell by about 15 percent. The recession of 1960 became officially recognized as such only at the end of the year. A nervous aftermath occurred in 1961, leading to the severe market crash of early 1962.

The odd thing about the 1962 panic in the stock market is that business started to rise at almost the same time as the 1962 crash started to happen. In other words, *businesswise* the recession was all over before the panic started.

6
Twentieth-Century Foreign Panics

Well, fancy giving money to the government
Might as well put it down the drain
Fancy giving money to the government
Nobody will ever see the stuff again
Well, they've no idea what money's for —
Ten to one they'll start another war
I've heard of a lot of silly things, but Lor'!
Fancy giving money to the government!

Sir Alan Patrick Herbert

FOREIGN TWENTIETH-CENTURY panics have mainly revolved around the aftermath of World War I, World War II, and the reverberations of the U.S. panic of 1929.

THE GREAT GERMAN INFLATIONARY PANIC
AFTER WORLD WAR I

While much of the world that had been involved in the war suffered inflation in varying degrees after World War I, the German example is the most famous. This is because it was the most dramatic. It was caused almost entirely by the unrealistic Treaty of Versailles which required retribution payments from the German people far beyond the capabilities of the economy of postwar Germany. It is probably reasonable to speculate that had the treaty never been enforced, the money fiasco would never have happened, and that the treaty not only crippled Germany for many years but created the atmosphere for Hitler to rise. The Allies won the war but certainly lost the peace. However, government currency mismanagement made the inflation infinitely worse than it need have been. Let us look at details.

In 1919, immediately following the war, prices in Germany rose about 50 percent, but by 1920 they were up about 500 percent. Some attempt was made to stabilize prices in 1921 and the rate of rise was cut to 40 percent. When there is a drain on an economy, be it forced or voluntary, the problems are great. It causes food for thought about today's U.S. military and foreign programs.

Between 1921 and 1922 the cost of living soared

another 500 percent. With prices once more rising fast, people rushed into commodities rather than holding cash. Shops were denuded of goods. This was hastened by the fact that the mark's exchange rate was rising faster within Germany than outside. The exchange rate for foreigners was extremely favorable. So not only Germans but foreigners too were buying German goods, because to them such goods were cheap. This added to the shortage.

This in turn promoted a tremendous increase in orders. People looking for "stores of value" were prepared to buy whatever they could. Of course some things were more attractive than others, and particularly the metallurgical industries had to work at full pressure, and with overtime to keep pace with the orders. The auto industry enjoyed a similar boom, if indeed it can be called a boom when the buying is artificial.

With money depreciating so fast, everybody was employed, but few people were making profits. It was harder and harder to get a good day's work out of a man. Wages in REAL terms were dropping (though rising in numbers) and with discontent on the shop floor, production slowed. Output per man-hour dropped badly. Incentive fell as prices rose.

Incessant disputes between employers and workers over wages caused increasing loss of time and production. There was a great increase in *unproductive* workmen. In 1913, for example, there were 66 unproductive for every 100 productive. By 1922 there were 120 unproductive. This was brought about largely by the increased need for accountancy with the swiftly depreciating currency. Also more people were needed just to negotiate and iron out labor and pricing problems.

Unemployment figures looked great but every

unproductive worker is as much a burden on the GNP as is an unemployed person. Production also suffered in another way. The entrepreneur concentrated his energies on goods and foreign exchanges in order to stay solvent, rather than concentrating on improving his product and reducing costs.

In the final year of inflation, in 1922/23, prices rose about 14,000 percent. When goods and services rise at that rate, prices lose all meaning. On August 30, 1924 the new Reichmark was fixed at one *trillion* paper marks to one gold mark.

THE OUTCOME

Soon after the inflation was over, George Halm, then a professor in Germany, ran a poll asking Germans which they would rather go through again — the war or the inflation. Without exception the answer was "the war."

It has been rightly said that an inflation to this degree, with the complete loss of the value of a currency, strikes a deeper and more widespread blow throughout a nation than virtually any other calamity. Families with a lifetime record of careful and prudent conduct saw their savings vanish almost overnight. The vast and class-proud German professional and middle classes were, in their own estimation, reduced to the standard of living of the industrial proletariat. The shock to the country's nervous system was only fully known years later.

The revaluation didn't solve the problems. The stabilization of the mark was assisted by foreign loans, which helped the government keep the parity. Also there were heavy cuts in government spending,

and a very sharp drop in interest charges. For a year
the German economy enjoyed a healthy recovery as
trade again got under way, but in the summer of 1925
unemployment again shot up to 1 million. A number
of the inflation-bred empires collapsed. Then in
1927–28 there was another surge forward. However
with the onset of world depression in 1930, Germany
was not yet strong enough to cope, and she suffered
very badly. Unemployment went to 10 million. Because of the hyperinflation there were now no middle-class savings, nor any business leadership, so
again Germany collapsed.

One must not forget the social chaos that the
whole procedure caused and the bitterness left in the
hearts of those who lost so much. It is the reason why
an otherwise quite sensible people were able to
ELECT a Hitler into power. Such is the destructive
power of inflation.

THE GERMAN STOCK MARKET

These days many analysts advise stocks as
hedges against inflation. Therefore it is well to spend
a few minutes examining the German stock market
during this period of 1919–1924, to see if those who
bought stocks really did hedge the inflation. The index, in terms of GOLD, fell from *69.3* in October 1918
to *8.5* in February 1920, although share prices increased rapidly.

Government securities, mortgages, debentures, etc., fell through the floor very early in the
procedure so the public began to think of shares as
representatives of intrinsic value. In 1919 a specula-

tive fury began. Even foreigners purchased German shares, speculating on the expected stabilization of the mark. Industrial and commercial firms tended to put their capital into stocks rather than in banks in hopes of saving some value. Shares passed from the hands of the investors to the hands of the speculators. It was entirely a speculator's market. Oscillations became more and more violent. New shares were continually floated because of the constant need for a new capital by industry. There was a permanent "liquidity crisis." Stocks ceased to be affected by *any* news, good, bad or indifferent, business or political, and were only affected by currency exchange rates.

Because of this, people who bought shares in 1920 actually escaped *some* of the currency depreciation, by buying with an already vastly overpriced currency. But had you bought shares in 1913 and just held them, by 1920 the loss would have been so great as to have virtually wiped you out, because the mass speculation started from the base of *real* value, far below the values of 1913.

In other words you had to wait to buy shares until the mark was already 20 times its former parity with the dollar before you bought into the market, if you wished to stay even or make a little profit, and of course assuming you still had some money left by this stage. That kind of timing could only be known in retrospect.

After February 1922 the market took a different trend, and by October 1922 the index in real terms was 2 percent of 1913 (a 98 percent decline) although of course *numerically* it was increasing.

There was another short, sharp, frenzied rise in stock prices at the very end, before devaluation. It

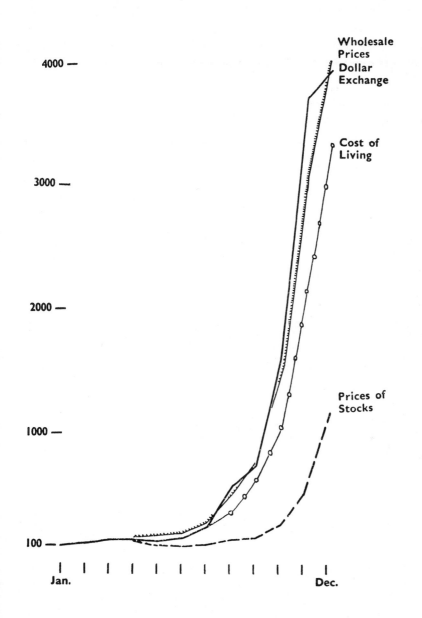

4000 —

**Wholesale
Prices
Dollar
Exchange**

**Cost of
Living**

**Prices of
Stocks**

3000 —

2000 —

1000 —

100 —

Jan.   Dec.

ry to December 1922, the height of the German inflation, showing how stocks went up
d not keep pace with the loss in value of the currency.

came in the final death-thrashing of the mark. By now there was no limit at all on the printing of money, and in the first half of 1923 stock prices did rise more rapidly than the exchange rate, with mining shares showing a preference. But of course to make money on this last leg one would have needed money abroad until this point, would have to buy in sharply, and then get out six months later just as smartly.

The average quotation for stocks one month after the devaluation was 26.9 gold marks. Had you held stock all through the fiasco you would have lost 75 percent of your value, which was a lot better than the local currency, but hardly a profit. From then on Germany was in a depression for two years.

In 1924 after the devaluation, private debt was revalued by legislation to about 15 percent of original gold value. Lenders thus lost 85 percent, sanctified by law. Government securities were revalued at 1000 old marks to 25 new ones.

THE REST OF THE WORLD AFTER WORLD WAR I

And what of the other countries torn by war? They too had their problems. By October 1923 the Russian ruble was worth one new gold ruble to 505 million old paper rubles, the Austrian crown 14,300 to one, the Hungarian gold crown 16,600 to one, the Polish zloty was 1,800,000 to one. Western nations fared better in most cases and prices had merely doubled. One may wonder if the seeds of the Iron Curtain empire were sown as early as this. It seems the chances of a country staying free after hyperinflation are very small indeed.

WORLDWIDE INFLATION AFTER WORLD WAR II

The magnitude of price increases from 1939 to 1948 are very similar in many countries to the price increases during World War I.

Australia, Venezuela, New Zealand, South Africa, and Norway had increases of 70 to 80 percent. West Germany, which had been hurt once, kept a tighter rein and thus had increases of only 44 percent despite losing a war.

In Canada, Switzerland, Costa Rica, the U.S., and the U.K. prices rose between 116 and 130 percent. In Czechoslovakia, Spain, Egypt, India, Chile, Palestine, Belgium, Turkey, Iran, and Brazil prices had risen 220–400 percent.

In Lebanon 674 percent.

In Bulgaria, Finland, France, Japan and Poland there were increases of several thousand percent.

When price increases get severe, the situation is made worse by flight from the particular currency.

Countries with super hyperinflation included Greece, Hungary, Rumania, and China.

It would appear that price increases of up to about 500 percent are often possible and yet under a *strong* government still containable. But beyond this point the government is swamped, and hyperinflation sets in.

In Russia the increase was in the realm of 150 percent. In China wholesale prices were trebling every year of the war. Greece experienced full hyperinflation and established a new currency in 1944.

It was of course with the backdrop of the above that the International Monetary Fund was formed. It was conceived "for all time," in an atmosphere of

war which looked like it would never end, and inflation that also looked like it would not stop. Once the
war was over, however, a worldwide deflationary period set in, in some places government induced, and
in others merely brought about by too much inflation, or from the effects of their major trading part-
ners deflating.

This ultimately led to the realignment of most
major currencies against the dollar and gold on or
around September 19, 1949.

But how was it possible to bring currencies
neatly into line? Answer: after a war people are prepared to endure much more than they will take at
other times. They were "conditioned" by stringent
controls and rationing which had been introduced
during the war and then kept on in peacetime as an
aid to "stabilizing" prices. Also there was no prosperity, as there is today, to be destroyed by deflation and
so governments met far less opposition with their
deflationary policies than they would meet today. By
the early 1950s prices had stabilized.

CHINA

China is interesting because the steps taken in
that nation form a classic picture of inflation. In 1935
a currency "reform" was introduced which took
China off the silver standard and on to a managed
currency.

This was brought about because of a rise in
silver abroad which drained the metal out of China.
(Sound familiar, re U.S. gold?)

Export prohibition proved ineffective; thus the
backing to her currency was being drained abroad

and by 1934 China had been forced to suspend cash redemptions on notes. With the help of an expert from the British treasury, the solution was to set up a managed foreign exchange backed currency.

The value of the Chinese dollar was set at U.S. $0.30. This was a 20 percent depreciation from the rate the Chinese government had managed to keep since 1934. The reform was to be effected by the surrender by the public of all silver. The silver would be sold to provide an exchange fund in foreign currencies to support the external value of the Chinese dollar. It didn't work.

Another attempt was made to reform the currency in 1942. It failed miserably.

By the end of World War II things were so bad that the use of silver, foreign banknotes, and U.S. dollars took over in many areas as the principal medium of exchange instead of Chinese money. Prices were often quoted in U.S. or Hong Kong dollars rather than Chinese dollars.

Those wishing to save during this period attempted to purchase gold and other precious commodities, or foreign banknotes or exchange. There was a flight from the money, as is always true in hyperinflation. Prices rose faster than the increase of the money supply, creating a permanent liquidity shortage and making the increase of the money supply more and more important. The rate at which the inflation moved is indicated in the following figures: The price of imported goods moved from an index of 198 in 1942 to 8,610 by 1945.

By 1949 a country that had housed an imperial family for centuries, that had truly lived up to the fantastic tales of Marco Polo, found that while it might have survived war, it could not survive war *and* inflation. The country was in chaos and the peo-

ple were starving, and so the people were ready for
a dictator. The communist peasant took over as their
symbol instead of the mandarin intellectual. The
time had come for Mao.

BRAZIL

Brazil is an enigma. At least on first glance.
Here is a country that inflated during World War II
and has been inflating ever since. Yet all those statistics that economists love, GNP, etc., look better for
Brazil than for most other South American countries.
Has Brazil proven that inflation DOES work? Let's
examine the facts.

First let's look at the rate of inflation. During
the 1950s Brazil inflated at a rate of between 10 and
20 percent per year. Compared with today's America
this hardly looks all that bad. In the early 1960s this
rose to 35 percent and more. With it came political
coups and dreadful sociological problems.

This is what makes inflation so lethal. It enables governments to bleed the country in every way,
and yet still make the statistics look good. Even
though the economic damage to a country is bad, it
is the social damage that makes inflation the worst
form of government takeover.

As we have shown in the German example,
unemployment figures can look quite good, and any
index such as GNP obviously must be adjusted to
cope with a depreciating currency. And who is to say
HOW it is to be adjusted? Why, the government of
course. In 1962–1963 the government permitted large
increases in the money supply and naturally prices

reached new and unprecedented levels. The cost of living rose 80 percent in 1963. They confronted the big unanswerable problem of inflation: how to stabilize prices without curtailing growth. By late 1963 and early 1964 a new problem faced them. Up to this point it was widely accepted that inflation was associated with growth. But now, on the one hand, inflation was accelerating and, on the other, growth was slackening. Prior to this time slowdowns had always been associated with anti-inflation policies. By the first quarter inflation had accelerated to an annual rate of 140 percent.

Again they were ripe for that dictator, and sure enough in 1964 there was a military takeover with Castello Branco becoming President. But the new regime fared little better, and by 1965 prices were increasing at an annual rate of 57 percent and business was stagnating. But since then inflation has been brought down to about 20 percent a year.

There is no need to relate the stories of terror and torture that are coming out of Brazil today.

ECONOMIC CONDITIONS IN BRAZIL

But what of the actual conditions in Brazil economically? Inflation over such a long period has *redistributed* the increment of the national product from the low-income consuming classes to the investment sector (both government and private). Government and its companies account for two-thirds of the country's capital formation. Government tends to work at cross-purposes with itself. For a long time government enterprises and the development bank's loan policy worked in such a way as to concentrate growth in one region. On the other hand the tax structure is designed to distribute income toward the less favored regions (right hand fighting with left hand).

Controlled prices are supposed to protect consumers against inflation. Yet monopolistic pricing or the price supports given by numerous government institutes to various primary sectors frequently result in a distortion of relative prices and a misdirection of resources and income, which the politicians then try to correct with government investment and subsidy.

Yet economists STILL point to Brazil and say inflation is necessary for growth, alluding to the fact that she has seemingly grown faster than most other South American countries. They fail to examine that she has more resources of manpower (85 million people) and geography than any of her South American neighbors, indeed more than most other Western nations. She has a very livable climate from a work point of view. Yet her people are lethargic. Could this be due to lack of real-value wages, that is, insufficient incentive? Also Brazil is still an underdeveloped country — 30% of its adult population can't read or write — and is formally classified as such. Her standard of living shows vast differences between rich and poor not seen in countries with more stable currencies.

In a permanent inflation such as this, people tend to make investments directly rather than through the capital market. Long-term financing as we know it does not exist. Investors prefer physical rather than financial assets, which might just disappear tomorrow.

RESULTS OF LONG-TERM INFLATION

The net result of this is that many excellent investment opportunities in Brazil are never filled. There is also a tendency for inventory investment and/or direct investment to be for relatively short periods. The type of industry that is likely to make a profit five years from now is of little interest.

There is a lack of interest in services such as power, transport, communications, etc., where there is a price-rigid economic overhead; and so the arteries of Brazil constantly break down and thwart business.

The incentive is to invest in flexible-price, quick-yielding sectors. Industry is completely at the mercy of inflation, and industries which require long maturation periods are sacrificed in favor of light industry. This of course slows down growth rate and is the main reason why we all run out of ideas after we have thought of coffee, when talking about what Brazil produces.

But certain economists say that if the inflation rate is constant and money supply is PLANNED to increase at X percent per year then people can plan accordingly. This has been disproved in Brazil. They have found no way (nor has anyone else) to keep the inflation rate constant; so it is difficult to predict the rate of inflation for a year ahead.

Over the years the trend has become more and more for government investment and less and less for private investment.

If you go into a shop in Rio, you will generally find that no article has a *printed* price on it, in the way we are used to seeing prices printed in, say, books that we buy. They wouldn't dare. In fact, in many shops there will be no price tags at all, just in case!

People don't want to pay off their debts. If they wait long enough then the bill, in real terms, will go down. Consumer goods, such as electrical appliances are well worth producing, because people buy such things as hedges against inflation. The rich send their money abroad, which of course is hardly healthy for any economy.

Real estate that can be bought on credit, particularly in urban areas, is popular. Most of the commercial buildings in Brazilian cities built since World War II are condominiums bought by the individual as a hedge against inflation.

When operating a business in Brazil, the first cardinal rule is "don't keep money on hand." Your assets must be in the accounts receivable and inventory. Stockholders don't want cash dividends; they prefer the company to plow the money back into the business and give out stock dividends.

Foreign investment in Brazil is far less than it should be, because of the currency problems. The following story of a U.S. firm explains why:

We had a good many millions of dollars in sales to this country during the years when inflation ran clear out of sight. We would deposit the proceeds with the central bank. By the time they converted the cruzeiros into dollars and gave us permission to remit the money, inflation had eaten most of it away. We lost 25 million dollars.

The biggest problem seems to be the businessmen's opposition to the curbing of inflation. The country went through a mild recession in 1965 and the rise in living costs was cut from 80 percent per year to 40 percent per year, but it was a recession in Brazilian terms and businessmen complained.

Politicians also find inflation a good thing. They can promise wage increases and subsidies. They can announce all sorts of public works projects, knowing full well that inflation will soon offset their grandiose figures.

II
PANICS
ANALYZED

7
Crises and the Business Cycle— Timing

Panics, in some cases, have their uses; they produce as much good as hurt.

Thomas Paine

TO UNDERSTAND crises and panics one must also understand the natures of business cycles, for the two concepts are interrelated. In fact, a crisis or panic is merely one short and dramatic phase or point in the overall cycle. It's that point where the bubble bursts, and where the human stampede begins.

One of the greatest myths in standard economic beliefs today, on both the private and the governmental levels, is that the business cycle is eliminated. This is complete nonsense. As long as ownership remains in private hands, and as long as investment decisions, based upon the profit motive, are made in the private sector, we will have business cycles. This system that we call capitalism is an inherently unstable one. There is a continuous tendency to move in one direction or another. And when we examine these tendencies statistically, a pattern emerges in the form of a cycle, the business cycle. (I'm not being critical of capitalism here, for in fact progress itself is unstable. True stability can only come with stagnation.)

It is today generally accepted that this overall cycle is really just a product of many subcycles, for cyclical behavior is common to many components of the overall economy. In order to understand and appreciate this phenomenon, it is very useful first to analyze some of these "smaller" movements.

THE PIG CYCLE

The ideal subject to start with is, of all things, pigs. It really does not matter whether they

The Pig Cycle

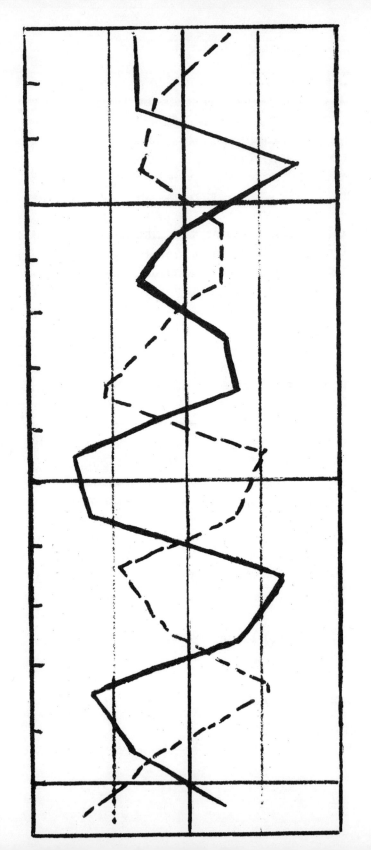

Source: T.J. Zimmermann
          Geschichte der theoretischen
          Volkswirtschafts-lehrs

--- Price
——— Supply

are American pigs, German pigs, or British pigs. The key to the cyclical phenomenon in this sector lies not in the color or size of the animal but in his keeper — the pig farmer. A human. As long as this human is allowed to operate in a free enterprise system it would appear that his reflexes in regard to pig raising are universally the same, regardless of nationality.

The discovery of this behavior pattern was made by a German statistician, named Hanau, shortly before World War I. He observed the following:

When the price for pork and bacon begins to rise at any given time, the immediate reflex of the farmer is to increase the breeding of pigs, to take advantage of the improved profit margins. Of course, each pig breeder thinks he's well ahead of everybody else in observing that great future profits must lie in this activity. But of course he is not. Pig farmers all over the country, in search of future profits, borrow money and all start breeding pigs like crazy. Pigs being pigs, it takes about one and a half years for them to reach maturity from the word "go." And inevitably, at that point in time, the pig market is flooded. As a result of oversupply, prices begin to fall. The margin between sales price and the cost of feed, etc., shrinks abruptly, so the pig farmers suddenly cut their pig breeding activities way back. All of them. In due course — measured again by Hanau at one and a half years — a shortage of pigs develops in the market. Prices once again start to rise. The margin between prices and the cost of raising pigs widens, and the cycle begins anew. This entire process is demonstrated in Figure I.

THE SHIPBUILDING CYCLE

Now these same principles apply in many
other sectors of the economy. Take, for instance,
ships.

When the Suez Canal was closed everybody in
the shipping business sensed a killing was in the
making. The necessity for tankers, and many other
types of ships, to go all the way around Africa in their
trips between Europe and the Near and Far East,
would create an enormous shortage of available bottoms. So rates exploded overnight, as everybody
rushed to reserve future space. And likewise, orders
for new ships flooded into yards all over the world,
from Japan to Norway. Come 1971, these ships having been built and delivered, the market was overwhelmed with capacity. Rates collapsed. Orders for
new ships came to an abrupt halt. Shipbuilding companies, on England's Upper Clyde, in Ireland, in Germany, were forced to close their doors. But now you
can almost bet your bottom dollar that the ship owners have "overcorrected" — just like the pig farmers
— and in 1975 or 1976 a new shortage of bottoms will
develop; shipping rates will rise, new ships will be
ordered, and the entire cycle continued in future, as
it has for many decades in the past.

Notice one important difference between pigs
and ships, namely the *lead time* between the decision to expand production and the ultimate flooding
of the market. Pigs take only one and a half years to
"complete." Ships take much longer. Thus the length
of the cyclical oscillation will obviously be much
longer in the shipbuilding industry than in the pig-
breeding sector. One could go on and on with similar

examples, with coffee, with houses, with automobiles, but really the only differences will be the length (and dependability) of the cycles. They exist in each case. They're not precise and they vary, but they are helpful.

GENERAL THEORY OF CYCLES

Going from specific sectors to the overall economy, starting in the nineteenth century, economists gradually discovered general cycles. In other words, a cyclical behavioral pattern was discovered for the whole. In the year 1860 the Frenchman Clemant Juglar published his book *Des crises commerciales et leurs retours periodiques en France, en Angleterre et aux Etats Unis,* which proved to be a milestone in this area. He came to the conclusion that a general economic cycle, lasting eight to ten years, existed. In other words, each ten years the world could expect to go through the process of depression, boom, depression. Because his observations proved of some validity, this particular business cycle pattern has since been called the Juglar cycle.

The next major step to better understanding of how our economies work was accomplished in the early twentieth century. In 1913 the Dutchman J. van Gelderen, in his book *Springvloed; Beschouwing over industriele ontwikkeling en prijsbeweging,* observed that in addition to this ten-year cycle, a much longer one existed, extending over several decades. Another economist, N. D. Kondratieff, in his essay called "Die langen Wellen der Konjunktur," written

in 1926, described this cycle in detail, and thereafter
it has been named after him. It is also graphically
presented in Figure II.

Finally, also in the 1920s, two further "founding fathers" of specific cycles, named Crum and Kitchin, discovered a very short cycle — lasting for
around forty months. This particular movement pattern has since been termed the "Kitchin cycle."

TWENTIETH-CENTURY BUSINESS CYCLE

The overall cyclical behavior of our economy
is apparently the product of the combination and in-
teraction of these three (at *least* these three) cycles,
which have been put into a composite form in the
accompanying illustration.

The graph should be consulted, for not only
does it make the overall picture quite clear, but it
may very well hold a key to the future. If we lay this
"chart" over the calendar of the twentieth century,
assuming that our year "0" is in fact 1900, we see a
remarkable similarity between the "calculated" path
of the Western economy and the real path it has
taken. In the late 1920s the boom collapsed, and
moved into deep depression in the 1930s. The revival
began in the 1940s, aided of course by World War II,
and this boom has extended roughly to the present
day. However, according to our "chart," we are right
now "peaking out." Our business cycle road map indicates that we are approaching within a few years
a new major crisis, perhaps of 1929 dimensions, to be
followed by a long, hard road down. The key curves
to be followed are, of course, the long-term Kondratieff cycle, and especially the composite cycle.

and Crisis Points
(Calculated Path)

crisis & panic danger

acute crisis and panic danger

acute crisis and panic danger

crisis & panic danger

crisis & panic danger

acute crisis and panic danger

1900 1910 1920 1929 1930 1940 1950 1960 1970 1980 1984

4

1

3

2

127

Source: T.J. Zimmermann
         *Geschichte der theoretischen
         Volkswirtschafts-lehrs*
         —Dr. P.E. Erdman—unpublished paper

1. Kondratieff
2. Juglar
3. Kitchin
4. Composite of 1, 2, & 3

This approach should probably be taken much more seriously than most modern teachers of economics are willing to do. For it is quite interesting that the signs of economic disintegration have mounted suddenly and crassly since the begining of the 1970s.

The world monetary system blew up in mid-1971. The back of the postwar European boom, which lasted twenty-five years, was broken. The American economy entered the greatest period of economic uncertainty since World War II. The stock market in New York entered a period of wild gyrations. Thus, it is suggested that you keep the picture provided in Figure II in mind, when you ponder the possible future *course* of economic events, and especially *when* you should start planning for them.

Now let's take a look at crises and panics in relation to the overall business cycle, and think in terms of what causes crises especially. And here money and credit play the lead role, since they occupy the key position in our capitalistic system as it exists today.

Fundamentally, an upswing in the business cycle is brought about by an expansion of credit. To go back to our first example, it was what made the price of pigs start to rise initially. This credit expansion, matched by an expansion of money in circulation, also *sustains* the rise in business activity, as long as the former lasts. The key to such credit expansion lies with the banking system — banks ease borrowing conditions, lower rates, literally push money onto their clients, in order that they, the banks, can expand and make more money in the process. The explanation of this process has best been expounded by Mr. R. G. Hawtrey in a series of books, starting with *Good and Bad Trade,* published in 1913. He puts the merchant in the key "decision" position. For he realized that although you can give marvelous incentives, you can never force anyone to borrow money, and start blowing up credit in the process. He sees the daisy chain as follows:

1. The banks offer increasingly attractive terms and interest rates.
2. The merchant is induced to increase his stocks, because it is cheap to do so, and he sees a "killing" in the making.
3. This produces larger orders for the producers of the goods he requires.
4. Increased output leads to increased consumer spending, as money circulates to the work force and suppliers.
5. This leads to an acceleration in the depletion of the merchant's stocks.
6. This produces still more new orders from the manufacturers, which in turn further increases consumer spending, and a still further depletion of merchant's stocks. Etc., etc., etc.

In other words, as Gottfried Haberler has put it in his classic book on the subject, *Prosperity and Depression,* "A vicious circle is set up, a cumulative expansion of productive activity, which is fed and propelled by a continuous expansion of credit."

THE ACCELERATION OF CREDIT

There is a further accelerating factor at work in addition to credit expansion, namely, an increase in the *velocity* of money in circulation. When prices go up, and trade booms, entrepreneurs and merchants not only borrow more, they put all of their heretofore idle resources to work, like cash in the bank, their securities portfolio, and so on. Ultimately money then is exchanged faster.

All in all, upswings in the business cycle are a cumulative process. Once started they feed on their own momentum.

Inevitably, governments and the central banking system fail to analyze correctly a situation that has gotten out of control. Certainly they have excellent weapons at their disposal, such as the discount rate, or open market operations, to brake excessive credit expansion. But it is almost always the same story: too little and too late.

The brake to the boom also inevitably coincides with that time when credit expansion stops. In fact, as Hawtrey put it, "If the restriction of credit did not occur, the active phase of the trade cycle would be indefinitely prolonged, at the cost, no doubt, of an indefinite rise of prices and an abandonment of the gold standard." This is, of course, exactly what happened to the United States in 1971. The credit system had been blown up to such a degree, and domestic prices forced up to a point so out of line with the rest of the world, that America essentially went bankrupt and had to suspend the gold convertibility of the dollar. But even the United States government then realized that it could not let this mad process go unchecked. Thus wage and price controls were imposed. But this merely *disguised* the fundamental problem. What must happen next, as so many times in the past, is that the banking system will be forced to stop expansion, and even to contract. This will happen when fears of a further "stagflation" reduce both demand (from the private sector) and supply (from the public sector).

At exactly this point, the super crisis is *bred*. And when the economy has peaked out, a process of contraction (which is *just* as cumulative as the upswing) is set into motion. A vicious downward spiral is the only outlook possible. And when this is sensed, at some time, in the financial community, there is a mad race for liquidity, for safety, for hard assets. And once this race is started, millions tend to join in.

The crisis then is the decisive turning point at the top. It is the phase in which many people feel that a decisive change, for better or much more probably for worse, is happening. It is a relatively short span of time where the feeling of insecurity is prevalent, and the expectation of possible catastrophe grows.

In other words, it is a psychological climax, based upon the end of a period of euphoria, which in turn was based upon an excessive buildup of credit.

This jumbo crisis may turn into a jumbo panic for actually no good reason. Mind you, it is fully possible to have an extended crisis in the business cycle sense, without having a panic. Panics develop purely out of human emotion, which is sparked off in an almost magical way. With a bang, the whole herd of sheep starts dashing madly in the wrong direction, fearing everything left and right. Panics often lead to disaster, for animals and for man. Panics are, by definition, irrational, the irrational reaction to the appearance of a crisis in the business cycle. For instead of trying to develop sound and rational ways to deal with the depression which looms ahead, people simply try to escape the future, by running.

Now, of course, the secret to survival in business cycles is closely related to being able to diagnose

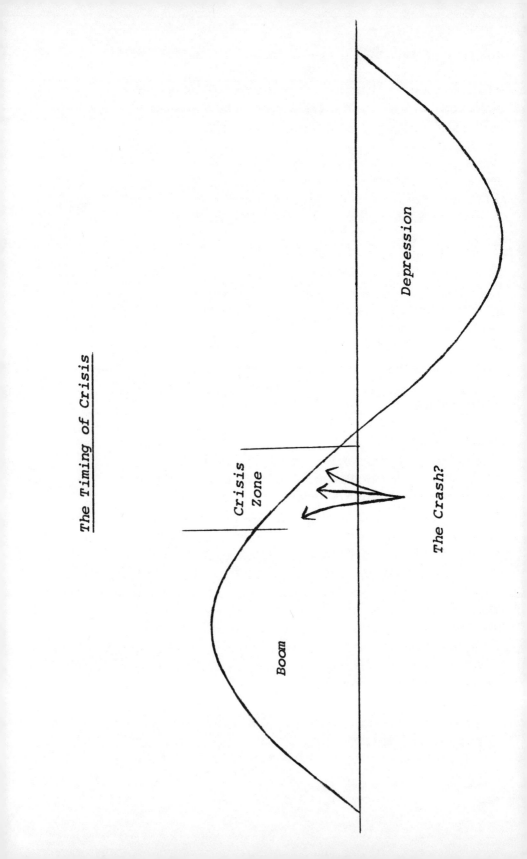

exactly where one stands, at present, in the cycle especially relative to the crisis which will inevitably come, and the panic which *may* happen in the crisis period.

So let's search for a few symptoms:

1. The length and speed of the upturn in which one finds oneself are of great importance. A business boom which has been going on for a great *number* of years becomes suspect by that definition. If it's starting to slow down it's even more suspect.
2. Credit expansion is a key factor to be watched. If one sees that, after a long period of excessive expansion and resulting inflation, suddenly the creation of credit is slowing — from either the demand or the supply side — look out! For the downward spiral of contraction is probably just around the corner. Increased credit *contraction* means the corner is at hand.
3. The acute corner itself, the panic, cannot be anticipated in any statistically systematic fashion. For it is to a good degree psychological in character. It can happen at any time in the period of crisis . Thus, if all of the other signs are ominous, it is probably best to watch the available emotional barometer with increasing care. Like: press comment, the behavior of the stock market, and even what the local merchant at the food store has to say.
4. Should everything start to add up, then the best decision is to run for cover. Rather be too early than too late. Trust your own common sense, that tingle at the end of your fingers, much more than the advice of your broker or even your banker. These professionals must stay optimistic to the end. You do not.

And for goodness' sake, don't fall back into the delusion that crises and crashes, and the depressions that follow, simply are not possible any longer.

The world is very funny. It likes to believe that current trends can be extrapolated into the future indefinitely. Thus in the 1930s the theory of secular stagnation was extremely popular in academic circles. This theory really said nothing else than that the world was doomed to live in depressed economic conditions, with high unemployment and a low employment of resources, forever.

Since World War II, this theory has been displaced by what one could term the theory of secular prosperity. We have been told time and time again that a depression, like that of the 1930s, can never happen again. We have been promised that there are so many "built-in stabilizers" in the system, that only pauses in, but never a reversal of, prosperity will ever be possible. (We will go into this myth in greater detail in the following chapter.) The theory of secular stagnation was completely disproved by events since its formulation. It seems equally clear that the current theory of secular prosperity will be proven just as misguided by future events. One can speak with confidence on this since, as already pointed out above, there are ominous signs that a long-term business cycle is now peaking out. And there is an equally ominous feeling in the air in the United States that a crisis, and perhaps a full-fledged panic, may not be too far off. So watch 1973–74. Even late 1972 may be in the danger zone. This will be the biggest "test" since the late 1920s.

8
The Government Ought to Do Something

If righteousness conflicts with the fancied need of business, then the latter must go to the wall.

Theodore Roosevelt, 1908

If two men had walked down Fifth Avenue a year ago — that would have been March 1933 — and one of them had a pint of whiskey in his pocket and the other had a hundred

dollars in gold coin, the one with the whiskey would have been called a criminal and the one with the gold an honest citizen. If these two men, like Rip Van Winkle, slept for a year and again walked down Fifth Avenue, the man with the whiskey would be called an honest citizen and the one with the gold coin a criminal.
                              Samuel Insull

THE BIG CRY these days is that "Government won't let another panic happen." So it is appropriate we examine this statement. The basis of this belief is of course that today we are different, that throughout history it is implied that business exploited, that business cycles took their toll, and government stood idly by and allowed this to happen. That today it is different, that government has learned to step in and take control to prevent the business cycle, and therefore we are on a permanent plateau of prosperity which will go on well beyond our lifetimes.

DO GOVERNMENTS INTERFERE?

If this is not so, then how did the myth of governments *not* interfering in the past come about? It came about because, as always, governments never take the blame for their own actions. While their actions did not exactly make markets fall day by day, their actions *prior* to the crashes, had CAUSED the crashes in most cases. In this chapter I hope to prove this statement.

The biggest thing that goes wrong with governments — the reason they fail to take the right action at the right time — is that in order to win popularity they have inevitably built into the economic system the seeds of its own destruction. Not only does the economy structure usually give too much to too many on the principle of "we borrow from tomorrow," but when things start going wrong, invariably government's answer is: "If we have run out of borrowing power from tomorrow let us borrow from next week instead."

With a system of total laissez-faire it is inevitable that the business cycle would be short and the fluctuations relatively minor. In other words, the uptrend would be mild for a couple of years, then would come a few months of stagnation, and the natural recycling would start again. This, while perhaps being a little inconvenient, at least would never be totally destructive, as for example 1929 was, BECAUSE government did something.

THE GOVERNMENT CAUSED 1929

Prior to 1929 government force-fed the economy for so many years after a normal reaction was due, that when the reaction *did* come (in spite of the government) only disaster could follow. And follow it did.

Also, because government did something in this century (1913) in the form of the Federal Reserve Act, it built into the system a means whereby the economy could continue to appear to prosper long after the setback should have occurred. This meant that the U.S. suffered far less from World War I than it should have. It also suffered less from the 1921 postwar depression than the rest of the world. But when the 1929 crisis hit, the entire country was plunged into total chaos and depression. The 1929 depression is probably the all-time classic example of the system whereby tomorrow is mortgaged in order to allow today's prosperity to reach unprecedented levels.

Without the Federal Reserve Act it is true to say that things could not have soared apparently upward on such shaky wings until 1929. The end would have come in a short, sharp burst long before that happened.

But then when 1929 was all over, nobody learned. Nobody blamed the system for allowing too much credit. Government economists blamed the brokers and banks for exploiting the law of lax money. They introduced the SEC which did not solve the problem of easy money; it merely victimized one section of the population against using it. This meant that from then on perhaps the bad credit structure could still be built up, but would not show up as dramatically in the stock market. It threw the burden of the weak link onto business and the credit houses. And it didn't work, because as 1937 showed, regardless of the built-in curbs, people panic.

In my opinion, prior to the more recent founding of the International Monetary Fund, the Federal Reserve Act in 1913 was the single most important and also the most unwise step government has taken monetarily. Therefore, we would do well to take a quick but closer look at it. It's not exciting copy but it is basic to understanding the structure. You may also be surprised at its cheek and naivete. It affects you in more ways than you may realize.

THE FEDERAL RESERVE ACT

The act was the direct result of a Monetary Commission study after the 1907 panic. Far from stopping any future panic, this act built into the American monetary system provisions which enabled the whole process of inflation to have official government sanction. From the Monetary Commission study it was evident that banking reform was necessary, but such was the blindness of the age that bank suspensions, that is, failures, were taken as evidence of a need for more lenient rather than stricter reserve requirements. Agitation centered upon demand for "more flexible currency." This thinly veiled cry for cheaper money was met by the act.

The common explanation for the institution of the Federal Reserve System is that the concentration of the banking reserves of the country into one institution permitted a greater mobility of these reserves. That by pooling the cash it was possible to use it, like a central fire station, to extinguish runs on smaller banks. In the words of one of its sponsors in 1914, J. Laurence Laughlin:

> The rigidity of credit banking in the past, the destructive snatching of reserves, are displaced by the system which allows good commercial paper to be converted into lawful reserves. . . . In time of panic — if any such arrives — there will be no reason for a run on cash reserves, or if there is a semblance of it, there will be a quick and ready way by which reserves can be replenished. There can be no serious run on the cash by the public, because the member bank can furnish at will reserve notes by making request for them at the Reserve Bank.

To bankers, the Federal Reserve Act meant employment of a larger proportion of total assets in the market place, hence with greater profit on bank capital; to the commercial community it meant easier credit, with money freely available, if not at lower rates, at least for more speculative ventures. A realistic appreciation of these factors, acidly written at the time, is that by the noted journalist C. W. Barron:

> The "motif" underlying the Federal Act is not that which is nominated in the bond. "An elastic currency" could have been enacted by 20 lines. The "means of rediscounting commercial paper" are already at hand and such discounts exist to the extent of at least 100 millions in the national banking system. It is not "to establish a more effective supervision of banking in the United States," for that could be accomplished by increasing the appropriation and enlarging the salaries of the examiners, so that men with larger experience and breadth of vision would perform more effective supervision.

To understand how the Federal Reserve System gave greater leverage to the inflation mechanism of deposit banking, it is necessary to outline the relevant provisions of the act. The act created twelve Federal Reserve Banks, each serving a separate geographical region of the country, and made them depositories for the cash reserves of the national banking system. At the time of the creation of the System much emphasis was placed on the note issue functions of the Reserve Banks. The banks were permitted in effect to issue legal tender notes against a combined security of gold and certain types of commercial instruments of debt, provided the gold proportion of the reserve constituted at least 40 percent of the total. Because of the growth of check-money and the expansion of deposit-credit, however, the real leverage in the money system occurred in the banking reserve requirements, and the manner in which they were manipulated.

1. The Federal Reserve lowered the reserve requirements against deposits. The national banking system had classified banks according to the size of the city in which they were located, as Central Reserve City Banks , Reserve City Banks, and Country Banks. For Central Reserve City Banks a reserve of 25 percent of total net deposits was required to be held in cash in the bank's own vaults; for Reserve City Banks a reserve of 25 percent of total net deposits, of which one-half might be held on deposit with designated correspondent banks; and for Country Banks, a reserve of 15 percent of total net deposits, of which three-fifths might be held on deposit with designated correspondent banks.

The Federal Reserve Act classified deposits into two categories, demand and time, with separate reserve requirements for each category. For demand deposits the act reduced the reserve requirements to 18 percent for Central Reserve City Banks, of which six-eighteenths (6 percent of total net demand deposits) were to be held in the banks own vault, seven-eighteenths to be held on deposit with the Federal Reserve Bank for its district, and five-eighteenths optional, either in the banks' own vault or on deposit with the Federal Reserve Bank. Reserve City Banks were required to maintain against demand deposits a reserve of 15 percent, of which five-fifteenths (5 percent of total net deposits) should be held in vault, six-fifteenths on deposit with the Federal Reserve Bank, and four-fifteenths optional. Country banks were required to maintain reserves of 12 percent against demand deposits, of which four-twelfths (4 percent of total net demand deposits) should be held in vault, five-twelfths on deposit with the Federal Reserve Bank, and three-twelfths optional. For time deposits the reserve was only 5 percent for all classes of banks. 2. In 1917, supposedly as an aid to floating government war loans, the reserve requirements were further relaxed, the proportionate reserves being reduced to 13 percent, 10 percent and 7 percent, according to the classification of the bank, with 3 percent for time deposits for all classes. The amendment provided that all reserve cash should be held on deposit with the Federal Reserve Banks.

Although under this amendment, till or vault cash could no longer be included as reserves, the amount of till cash required to meet daily withdrawals was small, so the result was an actual reduction in reserve requirements.

The effect of the amendment was to cause the banks to maintain smaller and smaller amounts of vault cash, in order to expand their operations to the maximum, and to rely on the nearby Reserve Bank for accommodation to meet sudden cash withdrawals. For instance, between June 1917, before the new reserve requirements went into effect, and June 30, 1930, net demand deposits plus time deposits of member banks of the Federal Reserve System increased from $12 billion to $32 billion but holdings of vault cash at the same time decreased from about $800 million to less than $500 million.

By making progressive economies in their use of vault cash at a time of rapid increase in their deposit liabilities, member banks were able to reduce their vault cash to less than 3 percent of their net demand plus time deposits by 1919, to less than 2 percent by 1924, and to less than 1.5 percent by 1930. In New York City, for instance, member bank holdings of vault cash in June 1930 averaged only three-fourths of 1 percent of their net demand plus time deposits and less than 1 percent of their net demand deposits alone. It was found that the practical effect of the 1917 amendment was to reduce reserves against net demand deposits from 18 percent to 14 percent for Central Reserve City Banks, and from 15 percent to 12 percent for Reserve City Banks with no change for Country Banks.

In 1924 the Federal Reserve System embarked on its famous easy credit policy, by reducing the rate at which it lent to member banks (the rediscount rate) and by forcing Reserve Bank credit into the banking system by heavy open market operations. It was not until 1928 that they became alarmed at what they had done, by which time it was too late.

GOVERNMENT MISMANAGEMENT IN THE 1930s

But what of the 1930s? This is the era when government did so much to "aid" the economy. The Keynes doctrine of inflation was adopted by Franklin D. Roosevelt as official policy. Gold was outlawed, and the American socialist era began. In the thirties, more than any other previous time in American history, government DID do something. Did it work?

In 1937 the stock market fell out of an apparently clear blue sky and in fact the whole of the decade of the thirties was more or less one of constant depression. The thirties should go down in history as a monument to government mismanagement and interference.

But what specifically did the government do

that caused 1937? While it is conceivable that they might not be able to get the country moving again, surely they cannot be blamed for making a bad situation worse. Or can they?

The market in 1937 became very "thin." That is the market which in the recent past had been capable of absorbing an immense volume of selling with only moderate concessions in price, had been brought to a stage where moderate selling brought about very large changes in price.

The causes for this thinness are found in governmental policies. One was the extraordinary tax rates and especially the tax on capital gains, which at that time was part of general income tax. Taxes for the upper levels of income had reached unrealistic levels. These rates applied to profits in the stock market and meant that men of substance simply could not engage in many stock market transactions. If they were successful, the government took most of the profits. If they had losses, they took these themselves. They now bought and sold only when they had a compelling reason for doing so. Moreover, the extraordinary high income taxes eliminated the current savings of men of substantial means, savings which had formerly gone into the stock market to a greater degree than other savings. The elimination of men of substantial means from the stock market tended to eliminate informed trading from the market. In the past, on bad days in the market, men with knowledge and buying power and courage would be on the lookout for bargains and would buy them. Even when the trend was downward such men acted as a cushion to the market. By 1937 the government had removed that buying power from the marketplace.

THE INTERNATIONAL MONETARY FUND

It was a war that America neither started nor
wanted, which finally pulled the country out of a
depression. It was most emphatically not government action that did it. Then in an atmosphere of
war, an atmosphere in which the world felt things
would never be the same again, America gave lead to
what I fear will prove to be the greatest monetary
disaster of all times: the creation of the International
Monetary Fund.

This fund has produced the same sort of easy
money on a global scale that the Federal Reserve Act
produced on a national level. At least two of its principal architects have since been proven to be communists, and while this does not make the whole
International Monetary Fund a communist plot, it
certainly does mean that some of the main beams in
its structure were based on the socialistic principle of
"from each according to his abilities to each according to his needs."

Whatever one's personal political views, the
fact remains that nowhere in the world has communism (or any form thereof) been proven an *economic
success.* It is not germane here to go into the political
ramifications of the communist architects of the
IMF; I merely wish to point out that, BECAUSE of
some of its originators, much of the IMF structure is
materially socialist in design, and so ultimately is an
economic failure. It has been an international engine
of inflation and inflation is only a label for currency
debasement. Destroy a currency and you erode a society.

It took 20 years last time for a socialist structure in the West, the Federal Reserve, to "bring the

chickens home to roost," in the 1929 crash. The International Monetary Fund has now been in existence about 25 years, and the signs of deterioration are everywhere to be seen. Most Western governments, however, while preaching capitalism and free enterprise, are still being "governed" by H. D. White and his friends, inasmuch as, instead of seeing that the basic structure was wrong, and so attempting to revert it to capitalist principles, they are merely injecting "more of the same." Those first architects could not have asked for a greater amount of success. It remains to be seen how the final debacle will be handled when it occurs. There are already powerful signs of a reversion to nationalism; while people will hang together in times of prosperity, it tends to be every man (or nation) for himself when things go wrong.

WHY DOES GOVERNMENT INTERFERE?

When suggesting that government should do something, we ignore the basic concept of business and free enterprise (and human relations and emotion). It is a fluctuating thing; progress is impossible without movement and, by definition, movement cannot only be upward. There has to be a pause for learning, for correcting error, for breath-catching once in a while. Left to itself the business cycle would probably ebb and flow in small waves at relatively frequent intervals. No government can stop this from happening. All it can ever do is alter the timing. For example, government may stop us having a minor recession every couple of years, one which we would barely notice. Instead, we get the recession in one big

glob every 20 years or so, and then we suffer for several years from it.

Why does government do this? To buy time. A
politician's first duty is to get elected. Thus when
things look slightly bad the politician feels obligated,
for self-survival, to cover up. That there are so many
advocates of the managed economy today is proof of
how well politicians sell the general public. But look
around the world and you will see that wars, dicta-
tors, and slump are among the "rewards" of a
managed economy.

WHY GOVERNMENT INTERFERENCE IS NOT THE ANSWER

I don't know if it belongs in this book, but I
can't resist the temptation to give an illustrative academic explanation for government's *built-in* inabil-
ity to solve problems. If it really *is* built-in, then the
best government is obviously the *least* government.
This provides the rationale for our claim that governments should return to the days of lesser central
control and activity and thereby return more power
to the individual.

First let me make four statements:

1. None of us is perfect.
2. We shall all make mistakes tomorrow.
3. We live in conditions of constant change.
4. There is no perfect way of serving any customer.

If all four of these statements are true then
there is only one method to find the best way to solve
any problem, and that is via *competition.*

Most governments give their people little or no

choice. They therefore *misuse* money and resources. As governments grow bigger and spend a larger percentage of GNP, and as they tax a higher percentage of income, their inefficiency grows. Imperfect man needs a regulating mechanism.

Free enterprise does this admirably. Competition enables the businessman to constantly check his premises against his competition to see whether what he believes (and does) really works. If it doesn't, then either he goes under or, if he is clever, he will change his ways and go on to meet the competition's challenge.

Unfortunately, when government steps in, there is no competition to regulate government. Hence, no plan that government ever puts into operation can be tested by a competitor. There is never anybody standing by to prove that he can do it better and thus force government to recheck its premises. This means that an error in government policy is almost never eradicated, except by revolution, war, or depression — which obviously are pretty drastic ways to show that government was wrong. Competition is far less painful. It is also more responsive to the people — to whom, after all, the country belongs.

There have been brief periods in history when a government cut taxes, opened up free trade (as under Emperor Augustus of Rome, which led to 200 years of prosperity), minimized its activity, and made money backing stronger. History shows all too clearly (though men refuse to learn by it) that people enjoy more freedom and more independence and greater happiness when they have less rather than more government.

And thus when government presupposes to *rule* a national economy it becomes a giant and with it comes less contentment, less real income, less liberty — and the original point above was that government *cannot* successfully invoke true prosperity by managing and minding everyone's business. All history bears this out in tall stone tablets, and on punch cards too.

9
People Who Made Money in the Various Panics

*Capital is that part of wealth
which is devoted to obtaining
further wealth.*
Alfred Marshall

THERE HAS ALWAYS been a pale of mystery surrounding the operations of the most successful speculators in the stock market. Why this should be so is difficult to appreciate, for there is actually nothing so very mysterious about these men, nor is there anything supernatural in their activities or their success in making fortunes through their speculations. Apparently the mystery is entirely the result of a general awe of speculation and manipulation.

There is no great secret for market success. Correct methodology is well known and apparent, yet how few in past years have followed the rules of the game with sufficient ingenuity to take a place among the immortals.

There must be fewer than fifty men of all the millions who have participated in the market who are entitled to have their names inscribed on the honor rolls of this select group. Yet careful study shows them to be little different from Mr. Brown two doors down the street, or the man we chat with at the brokers'.

ALEXANDER HAMILTON

Although he apparently profited in no way himself, it might be said that Alexander Hamilton, first Secretary of the Treasury of the United States was the first American stock market operator. Hamilton's genius in solving the troubled financial affairs of the then youthful nation were directly responsible for the foundations of several of the great fortunes of the country, as well as for the beginning of speculation in securities as we know it today.

Hamilton's Redemption and Assumption Plan which he succeeded in pushing through Congress, after exchanging in trade one of his party's major measures, greatly enriched his confidants who had previously bought up (for a few cents on the dollar) much of the scrip with which the United States paid off its Revolutionary War soldiers. With the passage of Hamilton's bill, this scrip was redeemed at par, much to the profit of Hamilton's friends. This government paper, made valuable by Hamilton's financial genius, became the first security to be "traded" in Wall Street.

However, while the speculators of the nineteenth century make very colorful reading, with their intrigue, power, and raids (both bull and bear), they offer little that we can imitate in today's market. Let us therefore confine our analysis of the big money names of Wall Street to those of this century, when the market was a little more organized.

BERNARD MANNES BARUCH

His activities were marked not only by continued success, but were also illustrative of a particular type of operator of that time, in that he operated both for his own account and as agent for other prominent financial and industrial leaders, especially in the merging of numerous important concerns.

Baruch was first known on Wall Street in 1896 when he became a partner in the old banking house of A. A. Housmann & Company. He was only 26 years old at the time, but his ability had brought early recognition.

He soon became known as a close student of financial problems and was soon the confidential representative of many great financial leaders in important transactions.

When the American Tobacco Company became a monopoly in the tobacco industry before the trustbreaking days of Teddy Roosevelt, it was Baruch who conducted the market operation that brought control of Liggett & Myers Tobacco Company to the hands of a strong New York syndicate which consolidated it with American Tobacco.

The success which attended his efforts made Baruch a wealthy man in a very few years. His fame was as great in Europe as in America, and indeed he was widely considered one of the great internationalists of the century.

In 1912, at age 42, Baruch retired from active duty in Wall Street to devote his attention to the development and reorganization of railroads, principally the Wabash Railroad.

Baruch was always strongly bound up with politics. Woodrow Wilson appointed him to the Advisory Commission of the Council of National Defense. He became its Chairman of the Committee of Raw Material minerals and metals, and was in charge of purchases for the Allies during World War I. Baruch was a prominent witness in a government investigation into a "leak" that developed during the negotiations. Although he testified to having made a profit of $500,000 during the days of the leak he declared that his sales of stocks were not induced by advance information!

He was also appointed Chairman of the War Industries Board. Wilson also appointed him to the American Commission to Negotiate Peace, and the American Peace Commission. In politics Baruch has always been classed as a Democrat. He was a generous financial supporter of the party.

WILLIAM C. DURANT

This man dominated the greatest bull market of pre–World War II days — that of the 1920s. Durant was a rich man in 1905, broke in 1910, owner of General Motors Company in 1915. He lost his $90 million fortune in 1920. By 1924 he had again amassed $20 million.

On entering the business world with no money, he borrowed $1,000 and with a friend founded the Durant–Dord Carriage Company in 1886. This venture prospered and soon became the largest carriage-making concern in the world.

In 1903 he organized Buick Motor Company. In 1908, immediately following the 1907 panic, he formed the General Motors Company and in the next two years purchased Cadillac, Oakland, Oldsmobile and several other companies. Profits rolled in so rapidly that Durant was freely offered high credit for expansion of his concern.

In 1910 the bankers of the country faced a condition of panic, and his credit line was withdrawn. As a result General Motors passed from Durant to the bankers, and he had to start all over again.

This he did. He organized the Chevrolet Motor Company and when it began to return sizable profits early in 1915, he did an amazing thing. He offered General Motors stockholders the opportunity to exchange one share of General Motors for five shares of Chevrolet. He also went into the market and bought General Motors stock, advancing it from $24 a share to $558.

172 STOCK EXCHANGES IN 46 COUNTRIES

By October 1915 he had full control of General Motors. By 1920 Durant had accumulated a fortune of $90 million. Then General Motors launched an expansion program which Durant bitterly opposed. In the midst of the expansion, with the company $200 million in debt, the panic and depression of 1920 hit the U.S. Durant tried various methods to bail the company out, but they all failed and his entire $90 million was swept away in the process. On December 1, 1920, at 59 years of age, he walked out of General Motors. A month later he organized Durant Motors, Inc. The company was never a great success, however. He also created somewhat of a sensation through his spectacular operations in U.S. Cast Iron Pipe in the early 1920s. In 1929 Durant pledged himself to pay back to original investors any money they had lost in Durant stock.

His leadership in the great Coolidge bull market of 1924–29 was almost fabulous. He threw his own millions into bullish operations, and many millions more furnished him by the greatest pool ever organized, composed of 25 multimillionaires. Under his personal direction he bought for the pool, in 1929 alone, more than $1,250,000,000 in stocks, while the partners of the pool invested at least two or three billions in addition on his advice. By 1928 this Croesus of a pool came as near to being THE market as anyone probably has ever been. His approach was bullish and logical. The market was so huge that it was impossible to lead the advance with a single stock. It became necessary to plug up all the holes throughout the list, and that is just what Durant did. Stocks doubled and even tripled at his hand.

One night at about 9:30 in April 1929, a taxicab drew up to the White House. He was ushered into

President Hoover's office. He warned the President that the worst panic in the country's history was developing. He advised the President that the crisis would come if the Federal Reserve Board did not reverse its newly adopted policy of curtailing brokerage loans and security credit. The Federal Reserve did not change its policies, and the following month (May 1929) Durant sailed for Europe and the pool started to unload. Withdrawal of these funds was a blow from which the market never recovered.

JESSE L. LIVERMORE

This man, more than any other in this century, can be regarded as a pure stock market trader. His five fortunes (he was bankrupt four times) were all made purely and simply from market trading. His technique was always all-or-nothing. He was always prepared to risk his entire fortune on what he considered a good buy. He has often been called "The Bear of Bears," but this is a completely false title. Although he successfully did make money in panics and bear markets, there is no evidence that he ever headed a bear raid, and he claimed he did much better in bull markets than bear. He listed two major points for success:

1. Sensitivity to mob psychology.
2. Willingness to take a loss.

For the former, so that he would know what the mob was thinking and doing, he employed armies of statisticians to plow through books and papers daily to keep him abreast of the news.

ROBERT RHEA

Perhaps the best "model" of a successful speculator for the *average* investor in the market, is Robert Rhea. Unlike the others mentioned in this chapter his manipulations were not spectacular. Neither did he have ethically questionable government connections which could supply him with information. He was the son of a river boatline owner who became interested in Dow Theory, in fact, by force. His father was a Dow student and coerced his son to study the Dow technique.

However, as he grew older, his interest in stocks and Dow Theory increased. Although bedridden much of his life with tuberculosis and a pierced lung, he studied avidly and became a very successful speculator.

His story, as I've said, is not dramatic, but is plain commonsense investing, based on time-honored principles. In 1930 he wrote a book on Dow Theory, published it himself and sold 90,000 copies. You may remember that Hamilton proved the success of Dow Theory by clearly predicting the 1929 crash within months of it happening.

Because of the success of his book, Robert Rhea started an advisory letter. To begin such an endeavor when the market was plummeting and people were losing both money and interest in the stock market was, by normal standards, madness. But he had something of value to offer. Proof that he did indeed have sound advice to sell is shown by the fact that by 1938 his letter had 5,000 clients, for those days a fantastic total. It has been said that Rhea averaged a little over $400 gain for every $100 he lost. In other words he was no magician, but he was a prudent and practical man, who was simply right on balance, and when he wasn't right he knew he had to cut losses and get out promptly. We can all learn from Rhea. The greatest truths are terribly simple. In the main we need self-discipline to practice premises we are already aware of.

JOSEPH KENNEDY, SR.

Certainly one name that comes to mind when conjuring up images of those who made fortunes from crashes, is Joseph Kennedy, Sr., father of JFK. Precious little is known for certain about his activities. But he who understands bear markets can (and should) invest *with* them, not fight them. That's why I wrote *Bear Markets — How to Survive and Make Money in Them*. The techniques for shorting are not well understood, but apparently Kennedy had them clearly in mind. The reason few make money in bear markets is that man is an optimist by nature. He is thus slow to sell out and fearful to sell short. Yet it is logical to do so. Kennedy was successful at bear markets perhaps because he was a cynic and/or pessimist. His tour of duty in London as U.S. Ambassador to the Court of St. James is an illustration of this. He was so pessimistic that he told Franklin Roosevelt England could not possibly survive Hitler's attack. That cynicism was of no value in politics but was of great use in the crash of 1929.

Of course, ideally, one should not be a pessimist to make money in a crash or panic. Rather one should be a realist. But this is star-quality stuff in the marketplace. People seem only capable of being end-of-the-rainbow type optimists or Gloomy Gus pessimists. Neither is wise, for both make one too inflexible and thus unable to reverse postures when the bull or bear move ends.

THOSE WHO MADE MONEY
IN GERMANY DURING THE INFLATION

It was the profiteers and the middlemen, the opportunists, the men who could combine business with investment — in other words, buy up a company to control it — exploit it and sell it. The men who made money during the German inflation were clever speculators who combined their knowledge of business with the strategy of the bourse and high finance. Without inflation it is unlikely they could have been so successful.

Foreign exchange also proved a source of vast profits. These big profits were made importing raw materials, and by others in exporting, buying up huge quantities of German goods and selling them abroad, all of which was basically a *business* way of practicing currency arbitrage.

The great industrialists and speculators operated only in part with their own capital. It was far more profitable at a time of continuous depreciation to borrow other people's money. It became the rule of good management to contract as many debts as possible and repay as far ahead as possible with depreciated currency.

Great profits were also made by manipulators who bought and sold companies on borrowed money, enabling them to buy in fantastic amounts, because of the rapidly depreciating currency.

Hence, during this panic in Germany in the

early 1920s it can be said that the people who made money were the businessmen who were opportunists and speculators. There seemed to be no way of making much money solely in business or solely in the market. It seemed essential to combine the two operations. It's a premise that might have merit in the present monetary climate.

CONCLUSIONS

It can be said, I think, that very few people make and keep fortunes in the stock market alone. The stock market, and indeed all trading, whether it be foreign exchange, commodities, import–export business, etc., is basically a way of conserving capital and/or income, rather than making a killing. As brokerage house statistics prove, very few people make money on balance in the market, and in times of panic it gets doubly hard. Hence the *first* art is to use the market to protect your assets, rather than primarily to increase them. If you protect your assets when others are losing theirs, then you are gaining ground. Further, if you learn conservation of capital, the knowledge will make your trading more profitable. Thus *expansion* of assets will follow as a by-product.

In a panic or bear market it isn't even necessary to make money to come out ahead of the crowd. When you see things getting shaky, if you sell and go into cash (often into foreign cash if your own country's currency looks suspect), then you'll retain your assets while others lose theirs. Relatively speaking, this is gain.

THE TRADITIONAL HEDGE

The standard hedge that has been used throughout history against disaster (Americans tend to imagine that theirs is the first country to have experienced anything and thus think no prior rules apply) is gold in whatever form your country will allow you to own it, be it bars, coins, stock, or whatever. Gold is the backdrop against which monetary disaster is measured. It is the world's unchanging monetary yardstick. It is the standard of value that stays constant and against which other *things* fluctuate. Hence by buying gold in some form you are in effect freezing your assets at a given value and allowing all other things around you to fluctuate economically, knowing that ultimately no matter how far out of line they have become, things will be remeasured against gold, sooner or later.

Perhaps the normal concept of "profiting" from a panic is slightly askew. During times of panic, few people "profit." Those who do are often people who actually trade on others' disaster, perhaps even making the disaster worse in order to increase their profits. We are not much concerned with such methods here, but rather we are concerned with *preservation.* During panics and crashes, governments complain and whine about the bears and the gold bugs and the gnomes of Zurich and the foreign exchange men capitalizing on disaster, but in very few cases do such charges have merit. The incidence is rare.

Man has a strong survival instinct and, provided he doesn't panic along with the masses and provided his government hasn't brainwashed him into believing that if he goes down with them and their mistakes he is being patriotic, then he will take steps to survive.

Such action is human, commendable, and honorable. Government officials in recent years who condemn the speculator for making money when they (the government) make fatal errors should take heed of Germany during the 1920s when so few people made money that Germany totally lost her middle classes — her "money with responsibility" class. For many years after this rape of the citizenry, Germany had monstrous problems because she became a leaderless society. Hitler finally filled the vacuum.

(For more background on surviving during crashes, panics and inflation I suggest you consult my prior book, *What the Prudent Investor Should Know About Switzerland and Other Foreign Money Havens.* [Arlington House, 1970]. It devotes a large section to the criteria for judging a nation's state of insolvency and/or financial risk.)

10

How the Money Was Made: A Summary

It is not the crook in modern business that we fear, but the honest man who does not know what he is doing.
Owen D. Young

GERMAN INFLATION IN THE 1920s

Some men came out rich. Some are legends of power and wealth in Germany today. How did they do it?

Some made money on foreign exchange, either by simply putting money abroad, or else by speculating in currencies. Some bought up huge quantities of German goods and sold them at higher prices abroad (in effect playing arbitrage with the internal and external rate of the mark).

Great profits were also made by knowing how to exploit the banks wisely. Buying and selling companies became a sport. It was done with borrowed money to be repaid in depreciated currency, so one profited twice over. However you had to know what you were doing. The interest rates could have killed you if you were not expert, for the German bank rate rose from 5 percent to 90 percent. Short term loans rose as high as *20 percent per day* or 7300 percent per annum.

The art of incurring debt in itself became a means of making money. Because of falling values it was possible to buy controlling interests in companies on the bourse, reorganize them, bleed them, and then sell them: transactions of a magnitude that could not have been carried out if their shares were priced in real terms.

Entrepreneurs also put money in "iron and stones." That is, they preferred to make machines and build factories (durables) than to produce basics such as foodstuffs and clothing. Such is the topsy-turvy attitude in a major inflation that people starved while men built factories to preserve assets rather than produce basic necessities for the community. In fact, iron and iron goods were used most extensively as a hedge in Germany.

As usual in all hyperinflations the rich got richer. Mergers were numerous, to enable small companies to survive. Wealth and power concentrated itself into fewer and fewer hands.

THE MIDDLE EAST

The wealth in the Middle East is invariably put into Swiss Banks, not only because the sheiks don't trust their local banks on the corner, but also because they never know from week to week if they will be deported, top of the wanted list, or even assassinated. Because of this, and of course because their nations have permanently unstable currencies, the best place for money is in Switzerland. They tend to shy away from stocks and shares, being far more happy trading international interest rates through Swiss banks (that is, putting their money where it will bring the most interest, and change directions when something else looks better). They are of course also big buyers of gold.

IN THE U.S.

During the panics of American history, men have made money in things other than the stock market. Very few names are remembered as being able to make fortunes on the short side, Livermore and Kennedy being notable exceptions. Even Kennedy's activities were largely possible because there was no Securities and Exchange Commission during the 1929 decline. And when he later was appointed to the SEC board, it was he who curbed exactly the types of activities (raids, etc.) that partly enabled him to make his money.

Also, a number of American fortunes have been made by bankers, entrepreneurs, and speculators who, while claiming to have no unfair advantage, did have very close links with government and government officials. Of the rest of them, many who appeared to have no special privileges tended to make their money by "taking a holiday" when they saw trouble brewing. They got out of the market, into hedges, and currency, dollars and foreign exchange, and simply waited with infinite patience for things to get better.

FINANCIAL SURVIVAL IN BRAZIL

We have seen in earlier chapters how, if one had put money into the stock market in Germany in the early 1920s and held on, one would ultimately have lost a great deal of money during the inflation. However, there are people today who still insist that the stock market is the best place for money during modern-day inflation, and so let us spend a few minutes looking at the stock market in present-day Brazil.

The annual index of price of the Rio De Janeiro Stock Exchange shows what the stock market did in actual figures and the broken line shows the same prices adjusted into real terms. The picture speaks a thousand words.

It will be seen however that there were years that one could have made a little money, and I will attempt to explain why. Prices rose sharply in real terms in 1959–1960 as the direct result of the creation of automatic mechanisms which were built into law and encouraged firms to issue numerous stock bonuses to their stockholders, and this made the buying of stock look attractive temporarily. The only other drastic rise in stock prices in 1962–1963, was the result of a tremendous surge of money pumped into the economy. By definition this could only be a temporary palliative to stay inflation from reaching the superhyperinflation level in one easy step. Of course, as soon as the money pump was slowed even slightly, market prices in real terms dropped and did not recover again.

Perhaps the most bitter condemnation of the effect of inflation on the stock market is the fact that in recent years in Brazil stocks have been selling en masse well below the value of the real net worth of the shares. Prices on the exchange tend to fluctuate sharply, not on the basis of expected earnings. Rather they rise when credit is easy and fall considerably when money is tight. Thus the market is overly sensitive to fluctuations in liquidity and almost completely insensitive to real values of companies.

In Brazil today investors tend to prefer other types of investment to stocks and shares.

Debt is a constant government problem in Brazil. In fact a few years ago the government had to introduce measures to make people pay taxes ON TIME, because the art in business was to delay paying taxes and thereby gain on the inflation which would have taken place before the taxes were paid.

Annual Index of Prices, Rio De Janeiro Stock Exchange. Source:
Serviço Nacional de Investimentos and Fundação Getúlio Vargas

e solid line shows numerical increase in stock prices from 1956 to 1966. The broken line
ɔws approximate "real value" increase (that is, prices adjusted for inflation). Note that if you
ught stock in Brazil in 1955, in sheer *numbers* the price of your stock would have increased
vhat looked like highly bullish terms. For each $100 you made $3,281 numerically. However
real terms, adjusting for the numerous devaluations (or, as the Brazilians emphemistically put
"the increasingly expensive dollar"), for every $100 you invested in 1955, by 1966 you
uld have lost 25 percent of your capital.

So today Brazil operates and invests in much the same things that people in all inflations have done, in things rather than in intangibles, in foreign bank accounts, foreign currencies, in playing the quirks in the local tax laws, etc. Indeed it can be speculated with reasonable basis that the whole so-called South American "Latin temperament" of *mañana* and of "everything has a price and a bribe and an angle" can be related back to a monetary system that has been in a state of chronic inflation for more years than any other system in any other part of the world. If you will allow me to alter an old proverb about power, I would add that just as inflation can corrupt, absolute inflation corrupts absolutely.

When a panic in the market has started, it would seem to be a good rule of thumb that while inflation is under, say, 8 to 9 percent, then *currency* is a good bet. Once inflation gets over that percentage, then currency might still be a good bet, but *not* your own; try one with a lesser inflation rate! If inflation never reaches these proportions, then you are relatively safe in local cash, because even if you lose on devaluation, it is usually a lot less than you would lose by holding real estate for which there is no market; or stocks, which invariably have lost far more in real value than the amount of the devaluation; or bonds, which fall through the floor the moment a currency is suspect. Of course precious metals are also a hedge.

Worldwide X-factor

There is one element that can be seen in all the areas discussed above, and in fact in all crashes and panics — even in the less dramatic minor recessions and corrective price weakness. This is the emotional factor.

What tends to separate the men from the boys is control over one's emotions. People tend to *buy* when prices are rising and prosperity is acknowledged widely. They tend to *sell* when prices fall and fear creeps into forecasts for the future. To move against this herd instinct is the necessary ingredient.

"Buy when the blood is running in the streets" is an old quotation that summarizes this point. Opportunities exist as much in bad times as in good. Since fewer people have courage in frightening circumstances, there may indeed be *more* chances than when virtually everyone is like-minded and optimistic.

Great fortunes are often traced back to buying when the mass was selling, or selling short when a panic began or even before it began, all of which requires courage and emotional cool.

Admittedly the timing for such action is a vast subject in itself. One cannot start buying the moment a downswing begins. One must be enough of a student of mob psychology to know when the crowd is *discouraged* (not only fearful) to collect the big bargains of a generation. Selling (or shorting) at the start of a fall or buying after a great slide, before others have regained courage, are the two basic approaches to making money on panics and crashes.

But aside from working out the timing factors, the point of this *X*-factor discussion is to highlight the *need* for steeling oneself (in advance if possible) for going against the prevalent mood. This is very difficult to do, and very easy to talk about in advance. *Making plans,* however, is one way to bridge the gap, just as a general finds retreat easier to face if he has planned a retreat route in case he needs it. Thinking ahead, then, is one vital key to emotional control, the *X*-factor in making money when others are losing theirs.

III
PANICS COMPARED

11
What Panics Have in Common

All the perplexities, confusion and distress in America arise, not from the defects in their constitution or confederation, not from want of honor or virtue, so much as from downright ignorance of the nature of coin, credit and circulation.

John Q. Adams, 1829

WE HAVE EXAMINED the panics and crashes from the time the New York Stock Exchange was big enough to be called an exchange until the present day. We should now look back to see if there is anything that they all have in common, or is it just, as all "good" history books proclaim, that in 19XX there was an unexpected panic.

Obviously, by definition, a panic has to be unexpected to the majority of people. If it wasn't, then there would be no panic. People can act with reasonable logic and rationality during times when new events are presented to them gently. It appears, however, to be almost impossible for human nature to act rationally when events are unexpected and a situation takes on a shock value. At such times otherwise rational men act with great emotion, and therefore great irrationality. But even irrational acts can be predictable. There is a pattern even in irrationality. For example the woman who worries about her children unnecessarily may be irrational in doing so, but it can be predicted that she will worry when they are out of sight.

A major purpose of this book is to attempt to show you ways to circumvent the shock element of panics. This should enable you to act with greater rationality than the next man and to predict his actions with some degree of accuracy. By this means we hope to enable you to come out both richer in coin and in emotional security.

MAN'S BASIC INERTIA

So why are panics always "unexpected"? Perhaps one of the major reasons is that man is a creature of habit. He suffers from a basic inertia which makes it infinitely easier for him to believe that, when events are moving in a certain direction, they must continue to move in that direction, and so all news to the contrary must be mistrusted.

This is particularly true of bad news, because man not only likes habit, he is also incurably optimistic. However, to a lesser degree it is true that when bad times turn to good (as you can witness at the bottom of any depression), when the ideal buying point occurs, volume is so low that interest in the market is almost nonexistent. At such times people believe that things will never be good again. Here habit triumphs over optimism and is thus the stronger of the forces explaining why panics occur.

PANICS ARE MAN INDUCED

But to return to the panics and crashes of the last 200 years. The main thing they have in common is that they are "man induced." In other words, although, for the sake of economic definition, people talk of business panics, banking panics, and monetary panics as if they were quite separate types, in essence they are the same and all are forms of human mismanagement. The principal difference is the part of the economy the mismanagement strikes at. In the last 150 years the only nonmonetary reason for a panic is famine, and it has been more or less eliminated in the industrial world. Therefore, in theory, once famine had been eliminated and man had learned to counteract nature and acts of God, he should have reached a permanent level of prosperity. That permanent prosperity is the logical outcome is shown by the number of economists and government officials who proclaim that indeed we shall never have a depression again.

But Utopia hasn't happened, as the preceding pages have shown. In fact, just at the point when those who should know better are proclaiming loudest that a permanent level of prosperity has been reached, something collapses.

WHY HAVEN'T WE REACHED PERMANENT "PROSPERITY"?

So what has gone wrong? When we have more or less solved the famine problem which baffled our ancestors for several thousand years, why should we find ourselves in a situation whereby we seem to have merely exchanged one problem for another?

The answer lies in the rate of progress over the last 150 years. It is very easy to solve a problem, "all other things being equal." However, over the last 15 decades, the *rate* of progress has speeded up so fast that man has been unable to cope monetarily. And that brings us to the aspect which all modern panics have had in common. They have been induced by monetary mismanagement in one sector or another.

In the last century, the mismanagement was shared jointly by both government and big business. But in this century the mismanagement was taken over more and more by government. Because total control of money by government is relatively new, government says (with relatively little fear of contradiction), "We will solve the problem for you." However, if one examines the methods government is using, they are virtually the same ones that were

used a century ago, and the results appear to be working out in a similarly disastrous fashion.

Conclusions

A monetary system is like a mirror. It can only
reflect. It cannot *create* business. If business fluctu-
ates, then monetarily the economy should fluctuate.
Unfortunately most politicians believe that money
exists of itself, and they distort the image for awhile.
However, there has never been a case in history
whereby anybody ever managed to distort the image
permanently. Once such distortion takes place, it is
merely a matter of time before the façade collapses,
with painful consequences.

A panic exists because some power has tried to
iron out the undulations in business and in monetary
interchange. The strength of the power determines
how long the undulation can be held back. It is probably true to say that, left to itself, an economy would
have two or three years of prosperity with a minor
setback on the fourth or fifth year. This is reflected in
the stock market. For some rather socialistic (that is,
idealistic and unreal) reason, nobody in a position to
mess with credit and currency *likes* this cyclical
(natural and realistic) system, and therefore these
politicians endeavor to hold back the normal diges-
tion periods.

In the last century they were able to hold off
these setbacks for only a very short period of time,
because the economy as a whole was disorganized,
and also regulators had less power. But as this century has progressed, with more and more power being concentrated in the hands of government, and

with the economy becoming totally centralized, then periods of prosperity (and quasi prosperity) have become longer and panics more pronounced.

The other aspect that creates a panic is man's greed. Part of man's optimism runs wild. He is so sure that things can only get better that in effect he borrows from tomorrow to finance today, forgetting that tomorrow has to be financed too. The system might work if the borrowing were constant, but his greed or optimism grows geometrically, and the borrowing for today gets bigger and bigger. And so tomorrow's debt grows disproportionately and indigestibly.

In the past in the U.S., the outcome of all this has always been panic. Odds are that it will be the same in the future, unless the form of government changes. For in a total dictatorship panics are eliminated. The reason for this of course is that one has to have the freedom to panic. However, one can't assume that therefore all we need is a dictatorship to create permanent prosperity. This is clearly not so: witness South America. And the reason for this is that ambition also needs freedom to survive. If you curtail the right to panic, that same oppression also removes the impetus and incentive that allows man to pick himself up off the floor and rebuild. Hence in a total dictatorship you may not have bad panics, but neither do you have sufficient or healthy growth. You have a state of permanent economic stagnation. The tighter the reins of the central government, the less economic progress.

12
A Panic for Today

Fear always springs from ignorance!
> Ralph Waldo Emerson

AFTER DISCUSSING panics and crashes of the past, one is then faced with the current situation. A mass of contradictions are bombarding us from all sides. We are being told that things never looked better. However, we're also told we must all tighten our belts.

Is this current situation very different from the past? Is it more sophisticated, more complicated, and more complex? Or is it rather that, when one is living a situation day by day, it is very difficult to see the forest for the trees? Most likely it *seems* more complicated today than it will in a decade from now when we look back on the early 1970s.

I believe that today is in essence very little differient from all "overripe" booms of world history. Communications are faster, but in an odd way this fact is counterbalanced by the fact that BECAUSE news travels so fast and so copiously, people become satiated with news, particularly bad news. They probably react less violently, less responsively to it than they did in the past when they got news of the outside world less frequently and in smaller doses. We're becoming almost immune to all but the most dramatic tragedies and events.

NOT "ONE WORLD"

Some try to make a case (especially in the monetary area) that if the U.S. money mechanism bogs down or fails, every Western nation will also bog down. Therefore, they claim, we are all committed to hang together, for otherwise we shall all hang or fall separately and simultaneously. I think this is erroneous on two counts: We do not *now* hang together through mutual interest as much as it appears on the surface, and also, if the U.S. falls in quicksand it will not drag down the rest (if indeed anybody else at all), or in any case not as far down. Prospects for another panic hinge on these conclusions being valid to some degree. One could fill a book or at least a chubby chapter with these arguments alone, and in the end you would still have to decide for yourself, since opinion is involved here as much as fact. However, history has yet to show an example of nations sticking together for long on any matter. In my view it is academically fair to say international glue is an illusion, on any long-term basis.

Furthermore, these chaps always talk in black and white terms, and assume extreme postures. They say, "If the U.S. collapses so will everyone else." But there is no question here of the U.S. collapsing entirely. The U.S. has suffered devaluation and depression and wars and civil war and civil upheaval, and has grown stronger after each episode. The U.S. will devalue again (soon) and there will be money panic and a stock market crash of monstrous proportions, but it will not bring down the nation. No nation has ever perished through a crash. Even if we assume the U.S. is on a downward trend as a civilization (à la Rome), no single money panic, however disastrous it may be, will terminate the existence of the U.S., or anything near it. Just as Rome took a thousand years to fall, so may the U.S. take a hundred — if we assume the trend is similar and it is not reversed. And just as debasement of currency was one of Rome's weaknesses, no money panic as such can totally fell a nation, however much chaos it causes. At least that's the path of history so far.

My final thought in this area is that European nations are reaching the point where, to keep the international money system together, they have to pull U.S. chestnuts out of the fire increasingly and this is now jeopardizing their own stability. The international glue will come unstuck without warning when they feel they have more to lose by holding the U.S. dollar up than by letting it fall. Therein lies the greatest threat, a real one, one which will bring on (soon I feel) the biggest panic and/or crash in modern time.

PREDICTIONS

Getting down to cases, what of America today? Do we have (as some claim) the classic signs of monetary panic shaping up in the U.S.? I believe we do.

I believe that within the next year or so America will be faced with serious recession, caused by the overissue of currency, that is, inflation and stagnation.

The type of panic that occurred in 1929–32, although caused by the usual monetary mismangement, took a course that is not possible to retrace today. In 1929 government allowed the economy to take the brunt of the deflation in a relatively laissez-faire fashion.

But today, with increased socialism and greater government concern with popularity, particularly among the lower-income levels, government cannot (by law) and will not (by conditioning) allow the economy to drift. The infamous Unemployment Act of 1946 forces government to step in. Politicians also feel that they have to take action, even if their action is quite wrong, for they are instinctively in a position of trying to HIDE the mistake, first and foremost, and then only secondly trying to CORRECT it.

The net result could be a much longer drawn-out recession, although more gentle. Whether or not America will finally recover from it to regain her former vigor can only be assessed, at bottom, by rating the government then in power. Germany, for example, after wild inflation in the twenties, did not have the impetus to get off the bottom when the inflation was corrected. Thus the economy, in spite of Hitler's declarations to the contrary, drifted for two decades, until after World War II, when Germany finally found herself a leader, Ludwig von Erhard, who would let the business community get on with the business of business. He actually encouraged it to do so, and so the German economic miracle came about. On the other hand, countries in Eastern Europe who went through much the same thing as Germany in the twenties, also drifted in the thirties and are *still* drifting, because of continued government mismanagement.

I do not feel we face total *runaway* inflation in the U.S. today. The U.S. is too closely watched by the rest of the world to pull out all the stops. What will probably happen is that this stop/go policy — which is sliding America into the gentlest (but what could perhaps be the longest) recession in her history — will continue for many years. Either way, you'll still wake up one future morning and find yourself with a valueless currency. But, unlike in past panics, most people will not know how it came about, because the erosion will have been relatively slow.

ANOTHER 1929?

When looking back on 1929 and trying to liken it with today, many people make the mistake of trying to compare the bottom of the crash with today's conditions, instead of looking at what *caused* the 1929 crash and trying to compare that with today. Yet while the actual market crash started in 1929, the real crunch didn't come until May 1931, when the failure of the Credit-Anstalt, Austria's largest private bank, caused reverberations around the world.

In sheer stock market terms, a crisis had already happened, but this was mainly because of the excessive credit structure within the market. It can be said that had the margin requirements been the same as today then the violent crash from 1929 to 1930 might never have occurred, but the economic hell of the thirties would have happened anyway.

The number of people wiped out in that first bear market leg down was *nothing* compared to the later devastation which was caused by excesses *outside* the stock market.

We all tend to look at 1929 today and say "Ah, but it can't happen again, because of SEC regulations." Quite right, it probably can't. At least that arrowhead top probably cannot, but everything else *can,* because nothing else has been changed since 1929 in credit structure or human nature — which is at the heart of it. No government agency can regulate the nature of man.

One-quarter of America's working force was unemployed before the depression had run its course, and had it not been for the impetus that a world war brought, the American economy could have drifted much longer. Granted the stock market

in 1929 did decline much more rapidly and much
deeper (percentagewise) than it has done to date.
Nevertheless, in the 1969 decline, *four times* as
much money was lost as in 1929. You *still* think it
can't happen again?

And just as government officials erected tariff
barriers in 1930, they are doing the same today. In the
twenties personal debt increased over 50 percent.
Does that sound a bit like today's debt structure? It
isn't. That figure in 1929 meant that consumer debt
was about one-twentieth of what it is today! We are
infinitely more vulnerable.

So many people look at the crash of 1929 and
compare it with today and say the two are totally
different. It *is* different in the *course* it is taking, but
the basic causes, such as vast overextension of credit
and inflation, are much the same. The key difference
is that in 1929 the excesses in the economy were *allowed* to right themselves, and so it was over fast.
This time it could take much longer, because natural
forces are held in contempt by governments.

Recession is not a synonym for deflation, as
many people seem to imagine. A look at South America and her problems will show you this. There we
see that it is possible to have recession *with* inflation.
When an inflation rate is excessive it *creates* stagnation of business.

I believe that stagnation of profits in business
generally, largely caused by and maintained by the
new chronic inflation that has come to the U.S., will
continue for some time to come. This will also crip-
ple the currency, which in turn hurts trade, etc. It is
a vicious circle with no early end in sight. No dramatic climax either. No bombastic depression (yet)
and no hyperinflation. Just a miserable state of
limbo, neither heaven nor hades. A frustrating,

seemingly solutionless lifelessness that now seems to characterize the scene.

How long it will last depends upon how long the real solutions are sidestepped — these solutions which politicians these days tend always to avoid. Those solutions (in my opinion) include drastic tax cutting, slashing government spending viciously in all areas, repricing of gold by 200 percent, restoring backing and convertibility to currency, termination of foreign loans and aid, and discontinuance of subsidies to farmers and business, removal of currency controls (interest equalization tax, curbs on capital investment, etc.), legalizing gold ownership, and allied measures. If these seem unlikely to come to pass soon, then so is the end to the U.S. economic dilemma.

The best hope is that Europe will force the U.S. to take remedial action. This could cause a momentary panic and/or crash but it would be beneficial in the longer view.

DEFLATION PROSPECTS DIM

It seems generally that it takes wartime conditions to make deflation work when inflation has really gotten hold of a country. The controls necessary to make it work in a country like the U.S. are just not acceptable in relatively prosperous peacetime conditions. What happens is the invoking of a "stop/go policy" — a series of mini-deflations to keep the international bankers believing that the country is really trying to do things right, and so keep confidence in the currency. This is followed by reinflation in order to prevent or stop unemployment marches on the capital, excessive strikes, and a drop in government's popularity in polls. Or even blood in the streets, following wage riots.

I do not believe that Washington will voluntarily remove the water from the economy. They will try to slow the rate of inflation, not turn it backwards. At this writing they are NOT succeeding in doing even this.

Do I believe that hyperinflation is possible in the U.S.? It is barely possible, but true hyperinflation is most unlikely, at least in the foreseeable future, if historical example is any guide. It seems that it takes some violent drain on the economy to make hyperinflation happen. It also takes a degree of isolationism within a country. Although America seems to be moving steadily in this direction isolationism does not appear to be a drastic factor for the near future. The two world wars were enough to bring hyperinflation to many countries. A revolution can do it. Hence hyperinflation is unlikely in the U.S. unless any of the above factors unexpectedly come into play.

CAN GOVERNMENT DO ANYTHING?

The cry that the government can control an economy nowadays is a *totally unproven* concept. It is very easy after 20 odd years of prosperity to say government can control anything. However, when we look back on history we discover that panics and crashes of magnitude have often occurred a great number of years apart.

The last 30 years have been an era of unprecedented technological progress, sufficiently so that our ancestors, looking at this achievement, would feel sure that because we have progressed so fast and have done so much technically we surely *should* all be in a state of widespread and permanent prosperity.

Hence, far from government creating prosperity, we see with dismay that in spite of our mechanical progress, governments seem to have brought us to the edge of recessionary trouble and a monetary explosion. And this of course says nothing of a world that has greater poverty and starvation than ever before. International management of problems (via the UN, UNESCO, IMF, etc.) have only widened the poverty gaps. "Management" by political groups has, in short, become a growing disaster in itself.

It is tempting to speculate that perhaps if governments had left us all well alone instead, we might indeed be in an era of undulating, self-correcting, healthy and virtually permanent prosperity. Have you noticed what happens to a busy intersection when a traffic policeman suddenly steps in the middle to "direct" the traffic? Almost without exception his interference slows down the traffic flow. That typifies the role of government interfering with economic flows.

Obviously, with government standing in the wings, prosperity becomes a right, not a privilege, and not the natural result of unfettered free enterprise. It also means that many people have reached a point of feeling secure in *not* working today. The many poverty programs would have been unnecessary under a free-choice economy, because people would have been more eager to work, given incentive instead of subsidies.

CAN GOVERNMENT CREATE WEALTH?

Government *cannot* create wealth; it can only redistribute *existing* wealth. Only man of his own initiative can create wealth and he does this by taking risks, from the entrepreneur who gambles his capital in business right down to the casual laborer who works like a demon for a certain period, gets good money, then risks where the next day's pay is coming from. When government redistributes wealth, it not only reduces the incentive to take risks and work hard, but it also loses much of the wealth in sheer administration.

In the redistribution process we also lose a great deal of our freedom. The only way government distributes is by taking away from the "haves" and giving to the "have nots." The "have nots" in most cases *never* will have, even with government handouts, and whereas under a freer system they may have been persuaded to work for survival, once they are looked after and cared for, there is no hope. No hope for them or for society.

At the same time of course the golden-egg-laying goose is being killed because, with lesser rewards in store for him, the man at the top finds the gamble less attractive — and thus business stagnates.

Government creating prosperity? Surely the only thing politicians are able to do is guarantee that, however far we advance, they will upset our steady line of upward progress. They will interfere with natural correction, artificially maintain a trend (at painful cost), and ensure that every so often we have a major monetary/economic collapse.

IV
CONCLUSIONS DRAWN

13
How to Survive This One

One can survive everything nowadays except death.
Oscar Wilde

IN LATIN AMERICA the situation seems to be one where the rich get richer and the poor get poorer, and of course inflation keeps this phenomenon going. The upper 10 percent of the population own 45 percent of the wealth, and they have an unusual tendency to consume. They spend a large portion of their income on imported goods, because products from a healthy economy are usually of better value and better made. However, because of the inflation, even the richest people tend to consume 93 percent of their income. The rest they probably put away in foreign banks.

Inflation in Brazil has led primarily to investment in real estate and service industries, which have enjoyed abnormal growth. This is because, as the gap between rich and poor increases, the market increasingly is for the rich. Applied to the United States, this would mean the lesser rewarding kind of investment during excessive inflation would be a Sears, Roebuck type of operation, whereas a Saks Fifth Avenue type would fare better.

Capital flight is also a constant problem, which can, at a certain point, help cause greater inflation itself.

"Hard goods" are traditionally a prime inflation hedge because of the flight from money into things. People try to buy up things, such as good quality household equipment, machinery, buildings, and land, at what they feel will be lower prices than those soon to come.

While inflation is "creeping" however, money itself can often be the best investment, because of good return from high interest rates. But when the rate accelerates too much, then devaluation threatens and the risk factor is excessive. When inflation has hit 8 to 10 percent, the local currency is no longer a safe place for assets, although this is an arbitrary figure.

LIQUIDITY

The first key test as to whether or not you are prepared to survive a crash panic is *liquidity.* How much of your total capital — your personal net worth — is in cash or near cash? The rule of thumb to be applied here is that *at least* 50 percent of your assets should be in a highly liquid form. The goal to strive for is 75 percent.

The reasoning behind this should be quite clear. Think back to the end of the last great boom, which collapsed in late 1929. The man who had his savings in the mattress, or in a safety deposit box, watched the crash of 1929–31 with almost total equanimity. He did not have to join the panic on Wall Street, or desperately try to sell property when absolutely no demand existed. He found himself sitting high and dry, while everybody else was trapped with assets for which the market was rapidly disappearing. As the depression deepened, accompanied by deflation, the purchasing power of his cash kept rising and rising. And late in the 1930s, when the turning point was finally approaching, he was able to pick up the investment bargains of the century, because he had the one asset everybody was desperately seeking: cash.

But there are other tests which must be applied parallel to the liquidity test. One of these is the *safety* test — that is, the place *where* your liquid assets are kept. In these days of rampant crime, mattresses or even wall safes are no longer the place. Furthermore, it is hardly prudent to keep too many assets in a bank safety deposit box, since the loss of interest can add up very quickly (and it worries the IRS no end).

Short-term interest-bearing time deposits make much more sense. But this of course raises the question of what bank. Remember again the 1930s. Banks were going down like tenpins throughout the United States, and the prudent man who had sensed that a financial holocaust was pending found that although he had passed the liquidity test with flying colors, he had failed completely where the safety and dependability of financial institutions were concerned. So he also joined the long lineup of losers.

To be sure, today we have deposit insurance, which at least covers a limited amount of risk related to banking institutions. But one cannot help wondering whether, and at what speed, this insurance system will actually work, should a countrywide chain of bank failures develop. It has never been put to the test. In fact, the whole system is based upon the premise that bank failures will be few and far between. The chances are therefore very great, in my opinion, that should a major panic develop in the United States, the assets of thousands of weak banks in America will be frozen indefinitely. Their customers will receive solemn pledges that, in time, they will be reimbursed for the amount of funds insured. But it is highly doubtful whether those customers will see *any* cash for a long, long time. In fact, the reserves set aside for protecting you are a fraction of one percent of the assets covered, so the risk here, in my view, is frightening.

The obvious thing to do is to avoid small banks, for they are almost by definition weaker, especially in a crisis. By this I mean their ability to draw on additional capital to cope with a run is considerably and usually critically less than that of the bigger banks. The second thing you should do is to examine carefully the balance sheets of the large banks you do choose. They make boring reading, but I'm afraid it's necessary homework. Better than reading the fine print on their bankruptcy notice if things go badly. Banks with a very high loan-to-deposit ratio should be avoided like the plague. They have *your* money tied up predominantly in the exact fashion which you were trying to avoid — that is, loans to corporations and individuals who will be illiquid and not able to repay after a crash.

Another item to watch very carefully on the liabilities side of a bank's financial statement is the ratio of large international deposits to total deposits. For instance, a bank which tends to "buy" large amounts of Eurodollar deposits in the international money market is in an extremely exposed position. This volatile international hot money will leave the bank at the speed of light should a crisis develop. Such a bank will end up with no cash left over to pay *you* off. Some major U.S. banks have as much as 20 percent of their total deposits from such sources. In fact, if we were given the true details of their positions, I suspect that the percentage would be very much higher at times.

Savings and loan associations are another definite no-no. These companies have almost all of their assets tied up in the most illiquid form of all — property. Even the most optimistic person can hardly expect them to be able to foreclose on these properties and get back enough cash to be able to pay off depositors.

At the bottom of the heap, brokerage firms deserve mention. Lots of people are in the habit of leaving large cash balances — uninvested balances — with their stockbrokers. Following a crash, you can be almost dead sure that your money has gone that-away, often for good. In this regard we do not have to go back to the 1930s. The year 1969 provides all the evidence we need. Then, just a sharp reversal in the stock market — by no means involving any crash or panic — brought dozens of such houses to their knees. Even the key men in the New York securities business have since admitted that Wall Street found itself at the edge of a terrible catastrophe. Very little has been done since to improve conditions there. So, for goodness' sake, don't leave your cash lying around Wall Street.

In summary then, cash balances should be kept only at large banks, in banks with low loan-to-deposit ratios, banks with a very broad base of domestic depositors.

But there is a third test for survival in a panic. That is the *currency* test. As everyone discovered to his great surprise in 1971, the dollar is not a dollar. It is today worth much less in terms of other currencies than it was a year ago. This lesson the Latin Americans, the French, and the British learned a long time ago. Now it is also time that Americans learn to seek protection for their assets in *strong* currencies.

History has repeatedly shown that the value of a currency — its international value — will inevitably be affected by the onslaught of an economic crisis and panic. Often, to be sure, it is difficult to judge how great the time lag will be between the collapse of a country's economy and the callapse of a country's currency. The adroit investor, who has already passed our liquidity and safety tests at home, can, if luck and timing are on his side, hop and skip internationally from one currency to another, and achieve an amazing degree of protection for his capital in the process.

This is by no means just theory, for it was done in the 1930s with quite measurable results. At that time it was the Europeans who practiced this game successfully, since most Americans were still terribly naïve concerning international money matters. To show how it was done before, and how you can do it in the future, let's go back to the 1930s and suppose that you were living in England. You had witnessed from afar the collapse of the Credit-Anstalt in Austria in the spring of 1931. Then, news of the run on German banks reached you in the early summer of that year. Crisis was in the air throughout Europe. You felt sure that this infection was bound to spread across the Channel. So you decided to move out of Europe and to move your funds to New York, where things seemed to have quieted down after the crash of 1929.

Sure enough, just a few months later, in fact on September 20, 1931, Britain, in an attempt to stave off economic collapse, went off the gold standard, and let the pound sterling start to float down in value. This was the start of a process of beggar-my-neighbor, whereby one country after another tried to get a larger piece of international trade and commerce by undervaluing its currency through competitive devaluation. The objective in all cases: to export growing unemployment.

The move to the States and the dollar proved correct, for the United States held the dollar firm, and so did the traditional gold-block countries — France, Switzerland, the Netherlands, and Belgium. So at least your savings were safe for the time being. Their value had remained intact, with their purchasing power growing as deflation increased.

But then in 1932 came the election and Mr. Roosevelt and promises of the New Deal. The New Deal could only mean one thing to the prudent observer: government would go on a spending spree at home and join in the beggar-my-neighbor free-for-all abroad. So at the end of 1932 you decided to leave New York and hop back to Europe, to one of the traditional gold-block countries, Switzerland.

Sure enough, in 1933 the inevitable happened. The U.S. went off gold, the dollar floated down in value, and was repegged in 1934 after a massive devaluation. But your funds were still intact, this time in Zurich.

But before long things also grew ominous there. Unemployment soared in Switzerland as industry after industry found it impossible to compete in world markets with countries whose currencies had been devalued. Social unrest grew. The writing was on the wall.

So in late 1935 you decided to return to New York. After all, the United States had its devaluation behind it. Now, as a result of the dollar devaluation, you could get 50 percent more dollars for your Swiss francs than before. And the domestic purchasing power of these dollars was still growing, as depression and deflation deepened in America. Of course, in 1936 the gold block collapsed, and the Swiss franc fell with all of the Continental currencies.

To end this little story, when the turnaround finally started in 1941, your money was still in New York, and 100 percent intact. You decided to use it to buy IBM shares, and wait out the war.

You can be quite sure that a pattern much like this will evolve following the next crash, and the one after that. But next time, things will probably happen much faster because of electronic communications, computers, intelocking bank arrangements, increased sophistication among speculators — business and private. There will be a time lag not of years between devaluations, but of months, or perhaps only of weeks. So speed of movement will be of the essence.

One way to prepare for all of this is to set yourself up at a major Swiss bank. It has all the attributes of safety that one can desire. And it can offer you *all* the currency facilities you desire, under one roof. Actually you needn't move your money from one country to another. You can keep it in the same bank, merely transferring it from a dollar account to a pound sterling account to a Swiss franc account and then back to a dollar account — depending upon how the merry-go-round develops. Swiss banks, then, can provide a one-stop shop for passing all of the survival tests in the next crash.

But now what about other assets? After all, no one keeps *all* of his net worth in cash, or near cash.

REAL ESTATE

Obviously you need a house to live in, and selling it to get more liquidity in preparation for the crash might be overdoing things a bit. But one thing you should do. Pay off your mortgage on the house. In the precrash days of a economic euphoria, as we have seen, credit keeps expanding, banks are very liberal with loans, especially on houses, and the temptation is great to take advantage of the situation. But remember: you lock yourself into a long-term commitment on interest rates. At the height of the boom, you may willingly agree to 8 percent interest. A few years later, after the crash, market interest rates will have plummeted to half, or less — maybe three or four percent. And you will be stuck with the old exorbitant rate.

Debt is a fine thing to have during periods of high and rising inflation. Then you pay back the bank with dollars which are worth perhaps only 75 cents in terms of purchasing power. But debt in the period of deflation and depression which normally follows a crash can be a millstone around your neck. So pay it off. You might be the only man in town to whom your banker tips his hat in respect, after the worst has happened to everybody else.

Any other type of real estate, except for personal use, is a very poor thing to have following a crash. Construction, during a depression, grinds to a halt. Therefore underdeveloped land is subject to almost nil demand. Buildings of all types are thrown on to the market, as sellers desperately try to raise cash; as banks and insurance companies try to regain liquidity. An example of what will happen occurs regularly in America today, especially in economically depressed sections of major U.S. cities. There landlords find it better totally to *abandon* properties, than to pump money in to keep them up for renters who cannot pay their rent. What is true today in midtown Baltimore, Washington, or Chicago, can become a nationwide phenomenon tomorrow.

COMMODITIES

Commodities are another thing to stay away from, if you sense that a deflationary economic crisis is pending. First of all, commodities in general are very risky for the ordinary investor. Usually investors operate in the futures markets, on margin. They have 10 times as much risk as their down payment. Thus a 10 percent downward change in price wipes them out. Government studies have indicated that even during normal times the vast majority of private investors consistently lose money in commodity markets. My guess is that this will rise to almost 100 percent in a crash. Very few private investors learn to play the *short* side, to bet that the price is going down. They are trained to think in terms of growth, of capital gains, of high flyers, from their dabbling in the stock markets. And this Pavlovian response is inevitably carried over into the commodities market.

If you decide to use the commodity exchanges for hedging in anticipation of a crash, then for goodness' sake learn beforehand all about these markets: about the vast risks involved here. Learn especially how to play the short side of the market, for the prices of most commodities will fall during deflation.

The reasons are quite simple. In the deflation or depression that generally follows a crash, industrial action slows down immensely. Industry's demand for raw materials — copper, wool, cotton, zinc, iron ore — falls accordingly. In fact, often market demand drops quite precipitously, as companies fall back on their inventories for as long as possible. This leads to price collapses, sometimes fantastic ones. But this does not make it all that simple to operate at a profit in commodities. Often industry groups and professional dealers have vast vested interests in specific commodities. They get together and promote phony "recoveries" in the markets, and scare the small investor into covering his short positions. It takes a strong heart and lots of money to win in the commodities markets, even if you have spotted the right trend. So the prudent man will generally avoid commodities.

STOCKS

By definition, the stock market falls to pieces as part of the crisis and panic process. Quite obviously, if you have a large portfolio of stocks, you are a sitting duck. You can't possibly win. In fact, if you have bought stocks on margin, you may be wiped out completely. There's no use in repeating the gory stories of 1929, except perhaps for one anecdote: "If you see your Swiss banker jump out the window, follow him. You're sure to make money." But I would not plan on even that.

Again, as in the case of commodities, one can argue for the short side. "If you are sure a panic is on the way, short every stock in sight, and wait it out." The only problem here is that you must have an almost supernatural sense of timing. The chances are there will be false starts, followed by great market rallies. And you will find yourself holding a short position which is costing you a fortune in margin calls. Lacking a real fortune, your broker will be forced to cover for you, and your grand design will have ended in shambles. As this world goes, no doubt about one week after you were forced to cover your shorts, the market *would* fall apart. But all you would gain from it would be a few stories to tell your grandchildren, and they probably wouldn't believe you anyway. In any case, many grandchildren avoid poor grandparents, being generally more attentive to rich ones.

MUTUAL FUNDS

The case of mutual funds, as a hedge against crashes, is notable for its absence. Mutual funds are always long in the stock market, and usually have a very small cash reserve — 10 percent is regarded as wildly excessive. If you have bought a "Plan" for the acquisition of mutual funds certificates, you not only will be losing the money you already have invested, but could find yourself putting in good money after bad. It is, therefore, small wonder that the great era of growth of mutual funds is drawing to its close in America. People are slowly starting to realize that most such funds may offer the worst deal of the century. About the *only* stocks that will provide a hedge in times of crisis and depression are those of gold mines. And mutual funds don't buy these. We'll come to that in a moment, when the issue of gold is discussed.

HEDGE FUNDS

Hedge funds are really funny. I mean, their whole idea was to provide protection in markets that were moving down. They could play the long as well as the short side. So what happened in 1969–70 when markets were moving down, way down? They had the worst record on Wall Street.

The fault does not lie in the basic concept of hedge funds, but rather in their implementation. They were organized, promoted, and run by 29-year-old geniuses whose orientation was that stock markets generally went up. For that was all that their experience had taught them.

Thus it had to happen. They were long when they should have been short. Then when they panicked and went short, of course the market recovered and they found themselves way out there in left field. With your money.

But the concept is still valid. My suggestion: find yourself a hedge fund run by 71-year-old "doddering idiots." They have the experience that counts. And stay away from the Harvard Business School cum Wharton fellows who have everything figured. They identify cycles with washing machines.

BONDS

Bonds *can* be a good investment in view of a pending crisis and depression. At the end of a boom, the yields on bonds are normally quite attractive — eight percent or more — and on long life bonds the interest payments can provide a very nice source of income during periods of deflation and rising purchasing power of money.

But — and here is the hooker — what debtor will be able to service the debt, as promised, during a long-drawn-out period of depression?

Let's start with a few who will most probably not be able to honor their interest payments or, perhaps, even their capital repayment when due. First on the list are "dynamic" corporations, which have

issued scads of bonds to finance their growth. When
their turn comes, their "dynamic" movement will be
just as speedy on the downside. These are types of
companies which have continuously to raise more
money in order to pay off their debts from the past.
When, after a crash, this process is no longer possible, the entire house of cards collapses, and you
might end up getting back five cents on the dollar.

Now the risk is substantially less where bonds
rated AA & AAA are concerned. These will usually be
found only on established blue chip companies. Such
ratings mean the firms are better equipped to survive
crises.

Municipal bonds are in the very suspect
class. In depressions municipalities' income (taxes)
shrinks, as income in general declines. But their expenses often rise as they are forced to help the plight
of community residents out of work and in trouble as
a result of depression. They too will find it almost
impossible to raise money on the capital market, as
a result of the general financial collapse which follows a crisis. Those cut off first will be the municipal
bond holders. After all, they are assumed to be rich
capitalists, and thus best situated to survive financially. The same applies to all non-federal-backed
government debt.

This leaves us with federal government debt.
One can assume that such bonds will be the safest.
For in contrast to every other type of debtor, the
government can print money to pay interest, and
repay capital. This is also true of Treasury bills.
To be sure, if the collapse is total, even the federal
government could call for a moratorium on *all* interest payments and then force through a total
consolidation of its debt, at some ridiculously low

interest rate. The latter seems unlikely at this juncture. But such things and stranger *have* happened before !

So if bonds, then choose federal government paper or triple A corporate bonds.

CONVERTIBLE DEBENTURES

These are supposed to be the greatest investment vehicle to be invented in the twentieth century. The story is that they go up when the stock market goes up, but at the same time they have a "floor," since they are bonds, and will hold up with all other bonds at times of falling markets.

This theory was blown right out the window in 1969–70. Ask the people who held convertibles of LTV or Commonwealth United. In this age of corporation crisis, when a stock goes bad — really bad — it means that the entire viability of the corporation is in doubt. Thus the price of convertible debentures moves parallel to the related stock price — ALL the way down.

If this was true in the relatively harmless days of the late 1960s, how much more will it be true in a period of *general* business collapse.

There is one saving grace, perhaps. Some of these convertible debentures are printed on very colorful paper, and might represent a highly unusual way of wrapping Christmas presents. This will, of course, be true only if your broker or bank can find and deliver them to you, out of the chaos which will inundate all financial houses following the crash.

SILVER & GOLD

Silver is (sadly) no longer a monetary metal. It is today a metal, a commodity, just like copper, tin, or lead. To be sure, it is still used for the minting of some coins, but so are various other metals.

This means that the industrial demand for silver — from the photographic industry, from the electronics industry, etc. — will determine its price. As we have already noted, in the general depression which is assumed to follow a crash, industry will have to cut back its output tremendously. And those industries which are most reliant upon silver will be especially depression-prone. Luxury and leisure items, like jewelry, films, and cameras, will be the first to be hit. Likewise the demand for electronic components will fall sharply, not only as their use in TV and radio sets declines, but also as the government cuts back its military spending to divert more tax money to public works and the like, as in the 1930s.

This means that no matter how you cut it, the price of silver seems likely to fall following a crash. It is, therefore, not an investment hedge such as the type we are seeking.

But this is definitely not true of gold. Gold bullion, or the shares of high-grade gold mines, are almost ideal hedges in times of crises and depression. Remember, it was the only commodity whose price went way up — and stayed way up — during the Great Depression. Following the crash of 1929, because of a government guarantee, it remained steady at just over $20 an ounce. In 1934 the U.S. government raised its price by 75 percent to $35 an ounce. Thereafter it supported this $35 price through the rest of the grim years of the 1930s, when almost all other prices were falling apart.

This will be as true in the future as it was in the past. The onslaught of a new crisis and panic, followed by major depression, will most certainly be accompanied by a new era of beggar-my-neighbor, competitive devaluations. In recent years we have been told that gold is a relic of the past, and on its way out in the world monetary system. Of course, we were told this by politicians with a vested interest in money inflation — which is difficult to pull off under gold discipline.

But contrary to all the prior propaganda, when it came time for the United States to devalue the dollar in December 1971, it was forced to agree to do so in the *only* way possible: by raising the price of gold!

This entire adjustment in the value of gold and the related value of the dollar was made because the United States was no longer competitive in world markets, had relatively high unemployment, and saw a dollar devaluation via a gold revaluation as a nice way out.

When in the future mass unemployment and depression return to haunt the United States, you can be sure that the government will return to employment of the same "cure" that Roosevelt used in 1934 and Nixon in 1971. It will raise the price of gold, and once again devalue the dollar. Only next time it will be in the same percentage range as chosen by Roosevelt, and not the eight percent selected by President Nixon. The adjustment will match the economic conditions prevailing. This is why canny Europeans continue to hoard the metal. They know a good hedge when they see one.

Americans are (for now but perhaps not for much longer) precluded by law from buying gold bullion. But they can aquire certain gold coins (see appendix), and are free to purchase shares of gold-mining companies. Both belong in a hedged port-folio. (Though, with the state of modern art, maybe a gold bar mounted on a stand would pass as art.)

FOREIGN EXCHANGE

Sound foreign currencies are of course always a hedge, and a portion of one's assets in times of crisis should always be in other currencies, not just one, but several. Today, for example, the Swiss franc, English pound, and German mark might make quite a good combination. Change about as conditions change. You can of course earn interest on these currencies, in savings or time accounts.

In the last (rampant) stages of inflation one should not try to hedge but just get out of the offending currency completely.

One also has to hedge against controls. If you want to move money, do it now. It may soon be too late. Controls keep increasing, especially in the United States.

Many people think art is an investment hedge, but historically it has only been a dependable hedge in creeping inflation. Once the annual inflation rate gets over about 6 percent, prices tend to turn down, so it is very likely that we are seeing the top in art prices. The reason? With inflation comes a liquidity shortage that only gets worse.

CONCLUSIONS

The main thing to remember with all these is, even more so than with the stock market, never put your money in just one thing. Choose carefully. Spread your risks. It takes GREATER, not less, know-how to profit during bad times, for you are bucking the trend, not going with it. You must also do your homework BEFORE you speculate. Like becoming an authority on bonds *before* you buy any. Be an authority on gold coins; know which ones are already selling at the higher premium prices relative to what they were 20 years ago. The same with what money you have in banks. Study how to get the most interest on your money with the shortest-term commitment of funds, and so on.

The coming few years are not going to be easy or pleasant. Those who stay ahead of the game will be either professional speculators or clever people who have done their homework. You can be right about the trend of the market and yet buy a stock that goes down. You can be in the right hedge but the wrong section of it (that is, the wrong year coins, the wrong currency, the wrong mine) and you will watch your investment go down while the hedge as a group goes up. There is no substitute for knowledge. It is both power and security.

To be sure, all of us cannot possibly know all the intricate ins and outs of investment markets, especially if one moves into the international field. After all, most of us made our money by being involved in the process of making things, or selling things or services. Making money with money is an art that has to be learned, often the hard way. The prudent man will acknowledge this. He will go to experts for advice, even if he has to pay for it. In the end it will prove very cheap. One never gets something for nothing. This is probably more true in the investment field than in any other. People who try to skimp on the cost of good investment advice will probably find themselves losing tenfold through amateurish mistakes.

"For knowledge, too, is itself a power" —Bacon

A concluding thought. You need not panic during a panic, or crash to earth with your assets during a market crash. You can make a kind of *friend* of crashes and panics by understanding their nature. You can avoid the mental upset and the emotional trauma if you grasp the habit patterns, learn the clues. You can preserve your capital while those around you are selling in fear at a time when they should be buying — or buy in confidence at a time when the crash has barely begun. If you merely hold your ground while others are sinking, you become relatively richer. With descipline of emotion and knowledge of field you can not merely hold your ground but also make major capital gains.

It should also be pointed out that the investments recommended are good in almost any economic climate. In the unlikely event the panic is long delayed, your capital would still remain intact.

APPENDICES

Appendix A

PANICS AND CRASHES, 1809–1962

Year	Nations Chiefly Affected	Duration of Depression
1809	England, United States	2 years
1815	England	Approximately 2 years
1836–1839	England, United States, France, Belguim	7 years
1857	United States and most European nations	3 years
1866	England	About 1 year
1869	United States	About 1 year
1873	Nearly all countries	6 years
1882	France, England	5 years
1890–1894	England, Germany, France	4 years
1893	United States	4 years
1900	England, Germany, France	4 years
1903–1904	United States	About 1 year
1907	United States, Europe	1½ years
1914	United States, Europe	About 2 years
1920–1922	United States, England, Europe	Less than 2 years in the United States. Continued widespread depression in England and Europe.

1929– 1933	World-wide	About 8 years
1937– 1938	United States	About 1 year
1945	United States	Less than 1 year
1948– 1949	United States	Less than 1 year
1953– 1954	United States	1 year
1957– 1958	United States	About 1 year
1962	United States	About 1 year

Appendix B

Gold Coin Bibliography

The best book on the subject of gold coins as a hedge against the coming crash is Donald J. Hoppe's *How to Invest in Gold Coins* (New Rochelle: Arlington House, 1970). The following bibliography (© 1970 by Arlington House) is reprinted with permission from Mr. Hoppe's book. It's a mine of good information for the potential gold coin investor, and anyone interested in gold *per se*.

Records indicate that more than 2,000 books have been published in the United States during the last century or so that have a text devoted principally to numismatics. New titles in this field are now being added at the rate of 250 to 300 per year. Include the published works on the general subjects of money, investing, gold, inflation, etc., and the list would probably number in the tens of thousands. *Coin World* publishes annually a general bibliography of numismatic books, which contains several thousand items. The subject is extensive, but the following brief list provides a beginning.

ANCIENT, BYZANTINE, MEDIEVAL, AND RENAISSANCE GOLD

Burckhardt, Jacob. *The Civilization of the Renaissance in Italy.* 6th printing. Garden City, N.Y., 1965.

Hall, V., Jr., and Stearns, J. B. *Byzantine Gold Coins.* Hanover, N.H., 1953.

Ives, H. E. *The Venetian Gold Ducat and Its Imitators.* Numismatic Notes and Monograms Series, No. 128. New York, 1954.

Klawans, Zander H. *An Outline of Ancient Greek Coins.* 2nd ed. Racine, Wis.: Whitman Division, 1964.

Wear, T. G. *Ancient Coins: How to Collect for Fun and Profit.* New York, 1964.

CATALOGUES AND REFERENCE BOOKS

Breen, Walter. *Major Varieties of U. S. Gold Dollars.* Chicago: Hewitt Bros., 1964.

_____. *Major Varieties of U. S. Three Dollar Gold Pieces.* Chicago: Hewitt Bros., 1965.

_____. *United States Eagles.* Chicago: Hewitt Bros., 1968.

_____. *United States Half Eagles, 1839–1929.* Chicago: Hewitt Bros., 1968.

_____. *Varieties of Early U. S. Half Eagles, 1795–1838.* Chicago: Hewitt Bros., 1966.

_____. *Varieties of U. S. Quarter Eagles.* Chicago: Hewitt Bros., 1964.

Brown, Martin R., and Dunn, John W. *A Guide to the Grading of United States Coins.* Racine, Wis.: Whitman Division, 1969.

Burnie, R. H. *Small California and Territorial Gold Coins; Quarter Dollars, Half Dollars and Dollars.* Pascagoula, Miss., 1955.

Buttrey, Theodore V. *A Guide Book of Mexican Coins.* Racine, Wis. Whitman Division, 1969.

Charlton, James E. *Standard Catalogue of Canadian Coins, Tokens and Paper Money.* Racine, Wis.: Whitman Division, annually.

Charlton, James E., and Willey, Robert C. *A Guide to the Grading of Canadian Decimal Coins.* Racine, Wis.: Whitman Division, 1965.

Clain-Stefanelli, Elvira. *Select Numismatic Bibliography.* New York, 1965. (This book is a cross-index of almost 5,000 U. S. and foreign numismatic books, listed by subject.)

Friedberg, Robert. *Gold Coins of the World, Complete from 600 A.D. to the Present.* 2nd ed. New York: The Coin and Currency Institute, 1965.

Hewitt, Lee F. *Price Catalogue of Modern European Gold Coins.* Chicago: Hewitt Bros., 1969.

Schlumberger, Hans. *Gold Coins of Europe Since 1800.* New York: Sterling Pub. Co., 1968.

Yeoman, R. S. *A Guide Book of United States Coins.* Racine, Wis.: Whitman Division, annually since 1947.

――――. *A Handbook of United States Coins.* Racine, Wis.: Whitman Division, 1969–1970.

――――. *Catalogue of Modern World Coins.* Racine, Wis.: Whitman Division, 1968.

――――. *Current Coins of the World.* Racine, Wis.: Whitman Division, 1969.

COIN COLLECTING AND INVESTING

Bowers, Q. David. *Coins and Collectors.* Johnson City, N. Y.: Windsor Publications, 1964.

Clain-Stefanelli, Elvira. *Numismatics — an Ancient*

Science. Paper 32, The Museum of History and Technology. Washington, D. C.: U. S. Govt. Printing Office, 1968.

Clain-Stefanelli, Vladimir. *History of the National Numismatic Collection*. Paper 31, The Museum of History and Technology. Washington, D. C.: U. S. Govt. Printing Office, 1968.

Kopkin, S., and Roberts, E. W. *Paths to Wealth Through Coin Investments*. Lynbrook, N. Y., 1965.

Reinfeld, Fred. *Coin Collector's Handbook*. Rev. ed. New York: Sterling Pub. Co., 1963.

_____. *How to Build a Coin Collection*. 10th printing, rev. ed. New York: Sterling Pub. Co., 1965.

GENERAL HISTORY OF GOLD

Allen, G. *Gold, History from Ancient Times to the Present Day*. New York, 1965.

Green, Timothy. *The World of Gold*. New York: Walker & Co., 1968.

Paul, R. W. *California Gold, The Beginning of Mining in the Far West*. Lincoln, Neb., 1967.

Rist, Charles. *The Triumph of Gold*. Translated by Philip Cortney. New York: Philosophical Library, 1961.

MONEY, INFLATION, AND FINANCIAL DELUSIONS

Groseclose, Elgin. *Money and Man*. New York: Frederick Ungar, 1961.

Mackay, Charles. *Extraordinary Popular Delusions*

and the Madness of Crowds. London, 1841. Reprint ed., with a Foreword by Bernard M. Baruch. New York: L. C. Page Co., 1932; 11th printing, 1960.

Rickenbacker, William F. *Death of the Dollar*. New Rochelle, N. Y.: Arlington House, 1968.

_____. *Wooden Nickels, or, the Decline and Fall of Silver Coins*. New Rochelle, N. Y.: Arlington House, 1966.

Rueff, Jacques. *The Age of Inflation*. Chicago: Henry Regnery, Gateway Ed., 1964.

White, Andrew Dickson. *Fiat Money Inflation in France*. Reprint ed. Irvington, N. Y.: Foundation for Economic Education, 1959.

PERIODICALS

The following newspapers and magazines devoted to numismatics are available by subscription, or at the larger newsstands:

The Coin Collector and Shopper (Monthly)
Iola, Wisconsin 54945
(Single copy 35¢)

Coin Prices (Every other month)
"A current guide to U.S., Canadian and Mexican coin prices, continually revised to obtain realistic and up-to-date values."
Iola, Wisconsin 54945
(Yearly subscription $2.00)

Coin World (Weekly)
P.O. Box 150
Sidney, Ohio 45365
(Single copy 35¢)

COINage Magazine (Monthly)
16250 Ventura Blvd.,
Encino, California 91316
(Single copy 60¢)

Coins Magazine (Monthly)
Iola, Wisconsin 54945
(Single copy 50¢)

Hobbies Magazine (Monthly)
1006 S. Michigan Ave.
Chicago, Illinois 60605
(Has a large coin section; single copy 35¢)

Journal of Israel Numismatics (Monthly)
Cliffside Park, New Jersey
(Yearly subscription $5.00)

Numismatic News (Weekly)
Iola, Wisconsin 54945
(Single copy 25¢)

Numismatic Scrapbook Magazine (Monthly)
P.O. Box 150
Sidney, Ohio 45365
(Single copy 60¢)

The Numismatist (Monthly)
Official publication of the American Numismatic
Association, P.O. Box 2366
Colorado Springs, Colorado 80901
(Single copy 75¢)

World Coins (Monthly)
P.O. Box 150
Sidney, Ohio 45365
(Single copy 60¢)

The following publications, though not specifically concerned with numismatics, do contain articles on international monetary developments affecting gold, domestic and foreign gold mining and production, legislation concerning gold, gold-coin and other treasure finds, and treasure-hunting techniques, all of which may be of interest to the gold-oriented investor:

American Gold News
(Monthly)
P.O. Box 427
San Andreas, California 95249
(Single copy 35¢)

California Mining Journal (Monthly)
P.O. Box 628
Santa Cruz, California 95060
(Single copy 40¢)

Appendix C

Inflation, 1914-1965

		Retail Price Indices 1914–65	1958=100	
	Britain	United States	France	Germany
1914	24	35	0.56	43
1915	29	35	—	—
1916	34	38	—	—
1917	41	45	—	—
1918	47	54	—	—
1919	51	62	1.34	—
1920	58	69	1.90	456
1921	53	62	1.72	536
1922	43	58	1.68	2,310
1923	41	59	1.87	1,613,345
1924	41	59	2.06	54
1925	41	60	2.18	61
1926	40	61	2.71	61
1927	39	60	2.96	64
1928	39	59	2.90	66
1929	39	59	3.12	66
1930	37	57	3.28	63
1931	35	53	3.18	58
1932	34	47	2.96	51
1933	33	44	2.93	51
1934	33	46	2.90	52
1935	34	47	2.71	53
1936	35	48	2.84	53
1937	36	50	3.48	53
1938	37	49	3.93	54
1939	38	48	—	—
1940	43	48	—	—
1941	47	51	—	—
1942	50	56	—	—
1943	52	60	—	—
1944	53	61	—	—
1945	55	62	—	—
1946	57	68	—	—
1947	60	77	—	—
1948	64	83	49	85
1949	66	82	57	91
1950	68	83	63	85
1951	75	90	74	92
1952	81	92	83	94
1953	84	93	83	92
1954	85	93	82	92
1955	89	93	83	94
1956	94	94	85	96
1957	97	97	87	98
1958	100	100	100	100
1959	101	101	106	101
1960	102	102	110	102
1961	105	103	114	105
1962	110	105	119	108
	Britain	United States	France	Germany
1963	112	106	125	111
1964	115	107	130	114
1965	121	109	132	118

Note: The two breaks in the German figures, in 1924 and 1948, indicate introduction of a new monetary unit.

Sources: **League of Nations** *Statistical Yearbooks. International Financial Statistics. Historical Statistics of the U.S.A.; Key Statistics 1900–64* (London and Cambridge Economic Service).

Appendix D

Inflation, 1940–1968

(billions of dollars)

YEAR	Private life ins. & pension reserves	Govt. Soc. Security & pension reserves	Savings deposits in all banks	Sav. & ln. deposits, Cr. Unions, & postal savings	Savings in cash & idle bank accounts	U.S. Govt. secs. held by indivs.	State munic., & corporate bonds held by indivs.	Mortgages held by individuals	TOTAL	Relative purch'g power of dollar	Annual percent deprec. of dollar	Annual loss of purch'g power
1940	29.7	7.4	26.5	5.8	13.3	10.6	29.9	12.0	135.2	99.0	1.0	1.4
41	31.9	9.3	26.6	6.5	14.9	13.6	29.0	12.2	144.0	90.2	8.9	12.8
42	34.4	11.8	27.1	6.7	21.5	23.7	29.7	12.2	167.1	82.7	8.3	13.9
43	37.7	15.7	31.1	7.7	32.7	37.6	28.1	11.6	202.2	80.1	3.1	6.3
44	41.8	20.7	37.6	9.1	43.1	53.3	26.1	11.3	243.0	78.4	2.1	5.1
45	46.7	25.8	45.6	10.8	53.2	64.1	25.6	12.1	283.9	76.7	2.2	6.2
46	50.5	29.4	50.8	12.4	48.7	64.2	24.6	13.1	293.7	64.9	15.4	45.2
47	54.4	32.9	53.0	13.8	45.2	65.6	24.2	14.6	303.7	59.5	8.3	25.2
48	58.5	36.4	54.5	15.0	41.8	65.5	25.7	15.8	313.2	57.9	2.7	8.5
49	62.9	38.8	55.6	16.5	43.1	66.3	26.2	16.7	326.1	59.1	+2.1	+6.8
1950	68.1	41.4	56.3	17.9	37.6	66.3	28.2	17.8	333.6	55.8	5.6	18.7
51	73.5	44.1	59.0	20.0	39.5	64.6	30.2	19.4	350.3	52.7	5.6	19.6
52	80.0	48.5	63.6	23.1	38.8	65.1	33.0	20.6	372.7	52.3	0.8	3.0
53	86.8	51.8	68.4	26.9	39.5	64.9	36.4	21.8	396.5	51.9	0.8	3.2
54	98.0	54.3	73.5	31.6	37.4	63.5	37.9	23.4	419.6	52.1	+0.4	+1.7
55	100.0	57.4	76.8	36.6	30.0	64.7	42.2	25.4	433.1	52.0	0.2	0.9
56	107.0	61.1	80.9	41.8	25.0	65.5	42.3	27.3	450.9	50.5	2.9	13.1
57	114.2	64.3	88.1	46.7	21.3	64.9	45.7	29.3	474.5	49.0	3.0	14.2
58	124.7	64.9	97.5	53.0	19.9	63.7	46.8	32.5	503.0	48.2	1.6	8.0
59	133.8	67.2	101.1	60.0	13.1	69.4	47.5	35.4	527.5	47.5	1.5	7.9
1960	143.4	70.6	119.6	77.2	10.5	66.1	50.2	38.0	575.6	46.8	1.5	8.6
61	156.8	71.7	120.8	88.5	8.8	65.9	51.7	41.9	606.1	46.5	0.6	3.6
62	164.0	74.7	139.2	100.8	6.4	66.1	52.5	44.0	647.7	45.9	1.3	8.4
63	178.2	79.0	155.3	115.7	0.9	68.2	54.4	45.9	697.6	45.2	1.7	11.9
64	193.7	84.4	175.8	128.8	1.0	69.7	57.7	47.7	758.8	44.7	1.1	8.3
65	209.3	89.7	199.4	140.1	1.5	72.1	59.6	48.7	820.4	43.8	2.0	16.4
66	214.9	95.9	213.8	145.5	2.0	74.7	63.6	50.4	860.8	42.4	3.2	27.5
67	235.0	107.2	242.7	156.2	1.9	74.1	66.8	52.1	937.0	41.1	3.0	28.1
68	250.0	115.5	268.0	165.0	2.5	76.3	69.8	54.0	1001.1	39.3	4.3	43.0

Appendix E

The Schultz Gold Portfolio

We suggest you buy all of these, or most, if possible. Trying to pick one or two winners from the group may be fun, but it's not good investment strategy. Mines are subject to unexpected setbacks (e.g. flooding and fire) which have nothing to do with logic or the general investment situation. Mining is a hazardous business, so spread your risk.

Note: all prices and dividends will be given in British new pence, since the prime market is made in London. If you want dollar equivalents, remember that (at time of writing) 100 pence equal $2.55. You may also tend to follow South African shares in terms of U.S. ADRs. ADR prices vary widely from those on the London and South African exchanges. (The first 10 are South African.) These variations, on both plus and minus sides, follow no logical pattern. In the end, the various prices inevitably come together again. The listing that follows is not necessarily in order of preference. We consider them as a group. (Prices, given for illustration only, are as of 1/13/72.)

1. *Hartebeestfontein.* Mining operations: This is a long-life mine (i.e., over twenty years life expectancy) in the Klerksdorf region. It has just initiated a merger with neighboring Zandpan mine. This should allow for

lower costs in joint mining operations and add a new source of profits from uranium. The gold ore is of a good grade at 15.8 grams per ton. According to the ever-cautious *Mining Journal,* Hartebeest is now "one of the more interesting gold-uranium investments." Current financial status: Hartebeest has 9 million shares outstanding. ADRs are available in New York. Share price at writing is 180 pence. The current dividend is four pence (of course, as with all South African shares, dividends are paid in terms of rands; we have converted into pence). The yield is thus 2.3%. The company is currently in excellent financial condition. Potential: our calculations indicate that at a $70 gold price, this mine will be in a position to pay an annual cash dividend of 40 pence. Using our suggested multiple of 10 to 12 times the future potential *dividend,* this would put the future share price in the range of 400 to 500 pence. As you can see, the capital gains potential is substantial.

2. *Buffelsfontein.* Mining operations: It has an expected life of twenty-five years. In addition to gold, it has a large uranium plant in South Africa. Recently it's been involved in heavy expenditures aimed at the development of deeper portions of its mining area; this has drained financial resources. But when the new areas come into full production, they should result in an excellent long-term posture. Current financial status: 11 million shares outstanding. ADRs available in New York. Current share price is 180. Pays an annual dividend of 9 pence, resulting in current yield of 5%. The company's financial resources are strained, but the current movement upwards in the free gold market should alleviate the situation quickly. Potential: The cash dividend potential at $70 gold price is 50 pence. Employing a dividend-multiple of 10 to 12 would put this share in the 500 to 600 pence range. Thus share price could increase by 250–300%.

3. *Elsburg.* Mining operations: this is a new mine in the West Rand area which is fast approaching full development. In 1973 it is expected to be milling high grade ore of seventeen grams of gold per ton. Estimated life expectancy: twenty-two years. Current financial status: Thirty-one and one-half million shares outstanding. ADRs available. Thus far the company hasn't paid a dividend, but it appears as if a 4 pence payout is just around the corner. The London share price is now 67 pence. The company is in good financial condition and appears underpriced by almost any standard. Potential: cash dividend potential is at least 10 pence. Some have put it in the 15 pence area, assuming a gold price of $70. Applying our multiple we get a potential price of 150–180 pence. But there's a risk factor. The nature of the reefs which Elsburg is exploiting is quite unpredictable. Nonetheless, a doubling of its price seems fully possible.

4. *Kloof.* Mining operations: Another West Rand mine. The current ore grade is 17.2 grams, expected to rise to 19 grams. This, plus the fact that the mine has a 40-year life expectancy, makes it one of the most interesting South African operations. It suffered recently from a major fire underground, but production is already restored 80% and a major insurance claim is outstanding. Current financial status: 30.2 million shares outstanding. ADRs available. The current dividend is 4 pence; the price is 247 pence, resulting in a 1.7% yield. This means the future is already somewhat discounted. The financial condition is considered excellent. Potential: assuming a highly probably monthly production of 245,000 tons of ore, a $70 gold price would probably mean a 30-pence dividend. The normal multiple puts the price in the 300–360 range, but due to the extraordinary life expentancy and quality of the mine, we'd expect to see this share at 400 pence or better.

5. *Western Areas*. Mining operations: adjacent to Elsburg in the West Rand area, this mine has joined with
its neighbor in a plan of development. Western Areas
has been milling relatively low-grade ore of 9 grams a
ton, but now they're going much deeper and the *Mining
Journal* forsees a "substantial improvement" in average recovery of gold. Mine life expectancy: 20 years.
Current financial status: 20.7 million shares outstanding—ADRs available. Current dividend: 3 pence; current price: 80 pence. Yield is 4.5%. Financial position
improving, with indebtedness scheduled to disappear
by 1973. This company seems unknown to most American investors. Potential: estimated dividend, at $70 gold
price, is 17 pence. Assuming a 10 to 12 multiple on this
future dividend, share price would be in the 170 to 200
pence range.

6. *President Steyn*. Mining operations. Located in the
Orange Free State, this mine is developing a major new
shaft which will in effect result in a new small mine
with relatively high-grade ore. Currently the ore is average grade, yielding 13 grams of gold per ton. It has at
least 20 years of high production left. Current financial
status: 14 million shares outstanding; ADRs available.
Shares now sell at 234 pence, with a 7½ pence dividend,
meaning investors have discounted part of the mine's
excellent future. No long-term debt. The dividend has
remained unchanged for 14 years, showing a rather
conservative dividend policy. Potential: At a $70 gold
price, the mine would be able to pay a 45-pence cash
dividend. Using our usual multiple, this means a possible price range of 450 to 540 pence.

7. *Loraine*. By some standards this mine, located in
the Orange Free State, shouldn't be included in this
portfolio, for the life expectancy is only estimated at 10
years, and the ore grade is only 10 grams a ton. But
there are very large tonnages of marginal ore accessi-

ble from existing shafts. Our guess is that 10 years is too conservative an estimate, especially in light of intermediate and long-term bullion price projections. Current financial status: 16.1 million shares outstanding; ADRs available. The current financial status is poor. In order to amortize existing long-term debt, they've been forced to suspend dividends. The current share price, 25.5 pence, reflects this. But with the current gold price over $45, short-term prospects have improved and financial recovery is definitely in sight. Potential: with a $70 gold price, this mine should be able to pay a 10-pence dividend. Due to the relatively short life-expectancy, it would be imprudent to apply our usual miltiple —5 to 7 would be more in line. This would result in a doubling to tripling of present share price. Though this share is speculative, we feel it belongs in our balanced portfolio.

8. *Vaal Reefs.* Mining operations: Located in the West Rand, this mine has a good grade of ore at 18.7 grams per ton. A merger with Western Reefs is under consideration. There are also good uranium facilities and ore. Current financial status: 19 million shares outstanding; ADRs. Though the company has a sizeable debt, its operations hold such great promise that this should create no problems. Current share price: 424 pence; dividend: 25 pence. Thus the yield is 6%. Potential: at $70 gold, this mine should be able to pay a 75-pence dividend. Due to the mine's extraordinary circumstances, we think the multiple should be at least 12 and maybe as much as 15. This would put the potential price in the 800–1100 pence range.

9. *Doornfontein.* Mining operations: This mine, located in the West Rand, has a good grade of ore, at 18.7 grams a ton. The life expectancy, 25 years, is one of the longest in South Africa. In 1971 it was plagued by rising costs, but better gold prices should amply com-

pensate. Current financial status: only 9.8 million shares outstanding; ADRs. The current London price is 162 pence; it pays a 11.5-pence dividend, thus yielding 6.6%. It has no long-term debt and appears to be in excellent financial condition. Investors seem to have cooled on Doorn due to publicity on its cost problem. This would have been justified if the medium term outlook for gold was $40, as many analyts have been assuming. But since December 1971 the name of the game has changed and so have Doorn's propects. Potential: at $70 gold, it is judged that the company could pay a 30-pence cash dividend. Employing our usual multiple puts the share price range at 300–360 pence. Thus we see the target at least 100% higher.

10. *American-South African Investment Company, Ltd.* Mining operations: ASA is an investment company owning mostly shares of South African gold mines. All but two of the mines already recommended here (Lorraine and Elsburg) are included. Current financial status: listed on New York Exchange; 2.4 million shares outstanding. Current price: $38; current dividend: 70¢. Thus it stands at an appreciable multiple on dividend payout. This is not really significant, however, as investors judge ASA on potential capital appreciation of the shares it holds. Possible vs. current net asset value is the key to ASA's performance. Potential: ASA's portfolio has, on average, an upside potential of 100–150%, in view of the probable reestablishment of dollar convertibility at $70 gold. ASA reached 82 in 1968. It wouldn't surprise us to see it back up there in 1973.

11. *Eagle Gold Mines Ltd. of Canada.* Though not in production, we think this is a good risk. Listed on the Canadian and Montreal Stock Exchanges, this mine has the largest proven and drill-indicated body of ore in Canada, if not North America. The ore is medium grade. The stock of this northwest Quebec mine has

been as high as $9; it now stands at $3. Production will probably start when the free market price of gold reaches $48. If our projections are valid, the stock is undervalued. It is traded Over the Counter in New York. We expect a price rise to $12 when gold is $70, a potential 400% gain.

Appendix F

Facilities Swiss Banks Can Offer You

1.   Simply "store" money for you, in complete safety. To many people who fear currency debasement in their country—or political problems—or whatever—this is justification enough. Switzerland's bank record for safety and longevity has no peer.

2.   Provide commercial "facilities" for business transactions anywhere in the world.

3.   Offer higher (credit) margin for buying stock, etc. than most countries.

4.   Give advice on worldwide investments (and especially European) with objectivity possible only through their neutral status, mid-Continent location, and centuries of investment precedent.

5.   Actually make investment decisions for you, keep your capital working on your authority to let them act for your account and of course at your risk (i.e. operate for you under power of attorney).

6.   Provide safekeeping facilities for everything from stock certificates to gold bars. However, because the Swiss value money, and husband it so well, it works both ways. That is, everything a Swiss bank will do for you, will cost you a fee, and usually the fee is slightly higher than you would pay in any other country for the same service.

7.   Make you loans on quality Swiss or US stocks. Gen-

erally a more flexible loan is available (i.e. percent of value) than elsewhere.

8.   Grant short and medium term credits to industry and commerce.

9.   Provide overdraft facilities for selected private and corporate clients (i.e. you can overdraw your account and pay interest on the amount overdrawn).

10.   Provide foreign exchange facilities in *all* currencies, not just the most popular ten.

11.   Discounting of Swiss and foreign commercial acceptances up to 180 days (financing of accounts receivable).

12.   Assist you in merchant-banking matters, such as mergers and acquisitions, corporate capital planning and reorganization, market-technical consulting, forming of holding companies, etc. Some banks will on occasion invest *with* you in a deal they arrange.

13.   Funds kept in Switzerland in Swiss Francs are unfettered and have unrestricted utility and versatility.

14.   Your Swiss banker's letter of introduction, given anywhere, carries more gravity, more weight than from elsewhere. He is more respected and letters are *not* casually given.

Types of Accounts Available

There is great variety within Switzerland, both in kinds of accounts and in rates paid, and it's always changing, but generally there are:

1. Swiss Franc "Deposit Accounts"—which pay depositors 3 to 4% interest at this time of writing.

2. US Dollar "Deposit Accounts." Often about 1% higher than the prevailing Swiss Franc rate. Range: from 0 to 6%, depending on money market conditions. Some pay 5% at time of writing.

3.   Regular account, which pays no interest. Usually called a "current account."

4.   Checking accounts in Swiss Francs. At a very few banks, interest is paid on checking accounts carrying a minimum balance.

5.   Checking accounts in US dollars. At a very few banks, interest is paid on checking accounts carrying a minimum balance.

6.   Investment accounts—which hold funds to invest in whatever securities are in keeping with policies of the bank and the general agreement of the client to either direct the bank or let the bank act on its own initiative via a power of attorney.

7.   Trust Account Deposits. Starting from $25,000. Three-and six-month investments, paying the maximum international rates.

8.   Fixed time deposits. Usually dollars and Swiss Franc amounts only. Will pay less than Eurodollar interest rate but tends to be in gear with it. Dollar accounts pay well above Swiss Franc accounts, since dollars are a higher risk currency.

Index

About the Author

Harry D. Schultz, Ph.D., D.Sc., was born in Wisconsin and raised in California. At one time he owned thirteen California newspapers, and was nominated for the Pulitzer Prize.

Today he publishes the influential *International Harry Schultz Letter*. Though this unusual investment letter is international in scope, it even offers advice on buying odd lots of stock. Dr. Schultz has written and published the letter in various countries; today he makes his headquarters in London.

Harry Schultz moves wherever the big financial and monetary news is breaking. His contacts include key people who make the news. Dr. Schultz reports that his readers include Richard Nixon, Enoch Powell in England, Jacques Rueff in France, and Samuel Schweitzer in Switzerland.

Dr. Schultz also organizes International Monetary Seminars that draw crowds here and abroad—despite the $500 fee. One financial reporter expressed amazement at what he called "this Schultz phenomenon"—a loyalty that enables Dr. Schultz to command what may be the highest consultation fee in the world, $700 an hour.

Harry Schultz's other books include *Bear Markets— How to Survive and Make Money in Them; Treasury of Wall Street Wisdom; The International Monetary Muddle; Handbook of Swiss Banks;* and *What the Prudent Investor Should Know About Switzerland and Other Foreign Money Havens,* and *Inflation and Inflation Hedges.*

ODYSSEY

OF A STOCK

The course

of the price of

General Electric

common stock, 1920-3